NATIONAL PARK MYSTERIES AND DISAPPEARANCES

THE PACIFIC NORTHWEST (OREGON, WASHINGTON, & IDAHO)

BOOK 3

STEVE STOCKTON

Copyright © 2021, 2023 by Steve Stockton
Published by: Beyond The Fray Publishing

This book or any portion thereof may not be reproduced or used in any manner whatsoever without the express written permission of the publisher except for the use of brief quotations in a book review. All rights reserved.

ISBN 13: 978-1-954528-20-8

Cover design: Disgruntled Dystopian Publications

Beyond The Fray Publishing, a division of Beyond The Fray, LLC, San Diego, CA
www.beyondthefraypublishing.com

BEYOND THE FRAY
Publishing

CONTENTS

Introduction   v

PART 1
OREGON

Chapter 1   3
MYSTERIOUS DISAPPEARANCES

Chapter 2   61
Haunted Oregon

PART 2
WASHINGTON

Chapter 3   75
MYSTERIOUS DISAPPEARANCES

Chapter 4   123
Missing in Olympic National Park and Forest

Chapter 5   137
Haunted Washington

PART 3
IDAHO

Chapter 6   145
MYSTERIOUS DISAPPEARANCES

Chapter 7   173
Haunted Idaho

In Closing   183

About the Author   185
Also by Steve Stockton   187

INTRODUCTION

Welcome back.

In this volume, we'll cover the Pacific Northwest, which has many strange disappearances, unsolved mysteries and murders, and possibly as a result of the former two, a few haunted locations.

In Oregon, we'll examine a few of the more than staggering 189 men and 51 women who officially remain listed as missing since 1997 by the Oregon Office of Emergency Management after trekking into Oregon's wildest places. Oregon also has more than its share of unsolved murders and haunted locations (Heceta Head Lighthouse, the Shanghai Tunnels, Lithia Park, Cathedral Park, the Elsinore Theater, and the Geiser Grand Hotel to name but a few).

Washington State has several clusters of missing persons, particularly on and around the majestic and iconic Mount Rainier. Some have even speculated that the mountain is "hungry," as it is such a hotspot for strange and unsolved disappearances of people who came here to never leave. The same is true of non-alpine accidents on the mountain. For example, a cargo transport plane crashed into Mount Rainier in 1946—and the bodies of thirty-two Marines remain entombed.

Washington is also home to serial killers and unsolved murders. Many UFO encounters have occurred here as well, most notably Kenneth Arnold's 1947 sighting, which kicked off the modern UFO phenomena. Washington State also has many reported sasquatch encounters, such as the Ape Canyon incident. It was here on Mount St. Helens in 1924 that a small cabin housing a group of miners came under attack by a gang of wild "ape-men."

Idaho has a fascinating (and growing) list of mysterious disappearances and cold cases from across the state. Strange unsolved murders, murder-suicides, and crimes of passion abound. From a paranormal standpoint, Idaho has been named the top spot in the United States for sightings of unidentified flying objects and lays claim to more than sixty reported bigfoot encounters. Reportedly haunted spots include the Twin Falls Courthouse, Morris Hill Cemetery, the State Hospital South Cemetery, Spirit Lake, the Jameson Hotel, and the Snake River Heritage Center, among others.

PART 1

OREGON

ONE

MYSTERIOUS DISAPPEARANCES

MICHAEL BRYSON – UMPQUA NATIONAL FOREST

DURING THE EARLY hours of Wednesday, August 5, 2020, Michael Bryson, twenty-seven, a resident of Eugene, Oregon, was last seen with friends at Hobo Campground near Dorena, Oregon, while partying with them.

It had been reported that he left the rave party at the campground around 4:30 in the morning and had not made his way back since.

Several months later, some of his clothes appeared in an area that could be seen from the road and was searched numerous times. Unfortunately, Michael remains missing to this day.

It is likely that Michael was the victim of foul play in the case, as his friends and family are baffled by it all.

What happened out there in the Oregon Wilderness? Misadventure, abduction or something else?

On August 4, he dropped by his parents' house in Harrisburg and told them he was riding up with a friend to Hobo Camp Campground for a weeklong birthday party.

Located in the Umpqua National Forest, Hobo Camp is a small, roadside campground located at the side of the road. It is described as "primitive," which is okay for a few nights' stay, but not somewhere you would want to camp for an extended period of time. It is located near a creek, accessible by a footpath.

As per Detective Richard Smith with the Lane County Sheriff's Office, Michael left his camping gear behind, his phone was turned off, and he hasn't accessed his bank account since he wandered off in an unknown direction.

Michael stood six feet tall, weighed about 180 pounds, and had short brown hair and hazel eyes. The last time he was seen, he was wearing a white T-shirt, tan shorts, and white Crocs with rainbows on them along with a corduroy baseball cap in a brown color. There were several tattoos on both of his legs, both of his arms, and his ribs.

Michael's last photographs were taken in the woods at a party that included music, drugs, and forty to sixty people. According to witnesses, Michael walked away from the campsite after he was last seen in a bus.

According to Michael's mother, "He got upset and walked off the bus and nobody has seen him."

A search and rescue team from the Lane County Sheriff's Office Search and Rescue was already on the scene, searching on land and on the water for any signs of the missing person.

There was no call to Michael's parents until 5 p.m. on the evening of August 6 about their son's disappearance.

"By the time we found out it was almost twelve hours since he had been missing. The moment I put my foot out of the car, I knew Michael was gone. People weren't looking for Michael. They were sitting around, drinking, eating, laughing—nobody was out searching for him, so I felt in my gut something had happened," said Michael's mother, Tina.

Michael's father, Parrish, weighed in: "There's been a lot of conflicting stories from the beginning. One story is that he walked away from camp. The other story is that a group of individuals picked him up on the road."

Over one hundred volunteers showed up to search miles of wilderness in the area. There were SAR teams searching the area on foot and on horseback, and drones were also used to scan the area from the air. A search was conducted in steep terrain with overgrowth and dense woods for nineteen whole days in a row. Despite that, there was no sign of Michael. According to Detective Smith, the case is a continuing and active investigation.

In total, the Lane County Sheriff's Office coordinated more than fifteen separate searches spanning two counties, and over seven hundred hours of paid and volunteer manpower had been logged.

According to Parrish Bryson, it seems the family never received any straight answers about Michael's disappearance from any of the attending partygoers. Rather, he believes they knew more than they had publicly admitted.

"The stories given by some of the people at the party are inconsistent. And most of those people left the day Michael went missing, and continued to hold raves and parties," he stated.

He also said that while many people had left the campgrounds, several friends, as well as a few strangers, had stayed to assist in the search. He adds "We stayed at the campgrounds for nineteen days looking for our son, and we're truly grateful for those who stayed and helped."

His son was just getting his life back together after a drug problem, Parrish said. Michael had worked at a local bar and grill before COVID-19, and he told his parents he was interested in becoming an electrician. However, he was often invited to DJ at parties and raves across the state due to his passion for music.

A little over six weeks after Michael went missing, his parents admitted to wanting to believe that he was still alive, but they feared the worst as well. "And he would never just leave. Even in his toughest times, he would always contact us. The idea that he would just disappear is unheard of," his father stated on the record.

The Brysons also searched the general area where Michael disappeared as many as three to four times per week, gathering possible leads and posting illustrated MISSING flyers at trailheads, bulletin boards, and at the campsite. "He did not just disappear into thin air," his father remarked to the press.

On December 11, 2020, a breakthrough occurred. A call came through from a person who believed that they had spotted something near Brice Creek Road, about a mile west of Hobo Camp and between Cedar Creek Campground and Lund Park Campground.

The Lane County Sheriff's Office and Search and Rescue teams were notified, and on arrival, these teams found some of the items of clothing that Michael was reported to have been last seen wearing. These items of clothing were found oddly placed near a swimming hole, even though it was in an area that had previously been searched several times.

"The blue-ribbon right there is where two of the items were found. And the blue and orange ribbon is where the other items were found," Parrish Bryson stated.

He continued, "I'm 99.9% sure that these items were planted. My gut tells me that they were probably placed there because I know the intensity of some of the individuals that went down through there. It's really hard for me to believe that they were there the whole time."

After the discovery, searchers continued to look for clues for a few days but found none. As of this writing in October of 2021, Michael Bryson remains missing, and there have been no further developments in the case.

SAMUEL SAVAGE BECKER BOEHLKE – CRATER LAKE NATIONAL PARK

. . .

IN THE EARLY afternoon of October 14, 2006, Sammy Boehlke, eight, was playing near the Cleetwood Cove area in Crater Lake National Park with his father, Kenneth Boehlke, forty-eight.

Sammy disappeared into the woods after running up a cinder slope.

Crater Lake National Park was established in 1902 and is located in southern Oregon. In total, the park covers 183,224 acres and includes Crater Lake and the surrounding hills and forests.

Many years ago, Mount Mazama collapsed, creating a nearly 2,148-foot-deep caldera that partially fills Crater Lake. The amount of water in the lake is replaced every 250 years by rain and snow, which offset the evaporation. This is the deepest lake in the United States, measuring 1,949 feet. For maximum depth, it ranks ninth, while for mean/average depth, it ranks third.

There are two small islands in Crater Lake. Located near the lake's western shore, Wizard Island is approximately 316 acres in size, while Phantom Ship, a natural rock pillar, is located near its southern shore. Because the lake has no inlets or tributaries, its waters are some of the purest in the world due to the lack of pollutants. There are relatively high levels of dissolved salts in the lake.

Due to its high elevation and influence from the Pacific, Crater Lake has a subalpine climate. Summers are mild and dry, but winters are cold and snowy, with average snowfalls of 505 inches per year and maximum snow cover of 139 inches or 3.53 meters. It usually takes until mid-July for this snow to melt. Even into the summer, hard frosts are possible. The surface temperature of the lake ranges from 33°F to 66°F. In the summertime, the lake temperature fluctuates between 50°F and 60°F.

As a result of the collapse of Mount Mazama, Crater Lake had no fish until William G. Steel decided to stock it in 1888 in order to allow for fishing. The fish were regularly stocked until 1941, when it became clear they could maintain a stable population without assistance from outside. Two fish species have survived from the original stocking: kokanee salmon and rainbow trout, with the salmon being the most abundant.

As part of its history, Crater Lake is also known for the "Old Man of the Lake," a full-sized tree that has been bobbing in the water for over a century. As a result of the low temperatures of the lake, the decomposition of the wood has been slowed.

Crater Lake is sacred to the Klamath tribe, Native Americans indigenous to the area. Generations ago, they told of it being the crossing point between Skell, a spirit from above, and Llao, a spirit from below.

Andrea Lankford, author of *Haunted Hikes: Spine-Tingling Tales and Trails from North America's National Parks*, writes this of Crater Lake: "... Llao and Skell fought gory battles here. Llao ripped Skell's heart from his chest, and Skell retaliated by dismembering Llao and throwing the body parts into the lake. Hideous monsters gobbled up everything but Llao's head, but the lake still holds Llao's spirit.

"When stirred, he may brew up storm clouds. When angered, he may appear in the form of a giant crayfish that climbs up out of the lake, snatches people off the rim of the crater that surrounds the lake, and drags them down into the water."

So now that we know what Crater Lake is, how it was formed, and what it represents to the indigenous tribes, let us look into the disappearance of Sammy Boehlke.

Despite his passion for life, Sammy was stubborn at times. Also, as a result of having a mild form of autism, he was terrified of loud noises and bright lights.

Sammie stood four feet eleven inches tall, weighed eighty-five pounds, and had short brown hair and brown eyes. The last time he was seen, he was wearing a long-sleeve black and green T-shirt, jeans, a blue coat, and red suede slip-on shoes with rubber soles.

While he had camping experience, he had no formal wilderness survival training given his young age.

At 4 p.m., the Boehlke family had pulled over at a pullout about five hundred yards east of the Cleetwood Cove parking lot area and were walking north along Rim Drive.

Sammy and his father were playing hide-and-seek on a graveled slope when Sammy saw some yellow that he thought might be gold. Sammy stayed on the slope, refusing to come down, as darkness approached and his father walked a short distance to the car to return to their Diamond Lake cabin.

Kenny Boehlke chased after Sammy, but Sammy stayed fifty feet ahead, likely considering it a game. "I never caught up with him, and at that point, he disappeared over the top somewhere and I lost him."

Within a matter of hours, more than two hundred people were combing an area of about six square miles, or four thousand acres. Dogs, helicopters, and heat-sensing cameras were used to search for the boy for a week, but he was never found. Authorities said a helicopter crew spotted some tracks, but they turned out to be animal tracks.

After that, the search continued intermittently despite heavy snowfalls in the area. Seven thousand feet above sea level, the park gets more than five hundred inches of snow each year. Although it was unlikely Sammy would have fallen into the lake because of obstacles on the slope, technical crews searched the slopes from the rim of the caldera down to the shoreline.

Participating in the search were SAR teams from Jackson, Klamath and Deschutes Counties, National Park Service searchers and trackers from California, Washington and Oregon. Mount Hood and Mount Rainier rescue teams were also involved, as well as volunteers consisting of employees from the BLM and US Forest Service.

It seems more than a little odd that a boy of Sammy's age, who was just "slightly autistic," would just run off into the woods without any reason at all and continue going until he was out of sight and hearing range of his father.

Because it was cold, his first instinct should have been to turn around and return to his father, especially if he was calling for him, no matter how long he hid from him. No trace was ever found, and Sammy remains missing.

ROBERT WINTERS – SPARKS LAKE

BOB WINTERS, seventy-eight, was on a hunting trip with his family around Sparks Lake in Oregon when he disappeared in October of 1969. Broken Top Mountain is located to the south, while Mount Bachelor is located to the north of the lake.

Over the past twenty years, Robert and his sons Charles, George, and Alvin had hunted in Oregon on annual trips. As a result of snowfall at higher altitudes, hunting in this area would have been more difficult.

Robert was last seen at around 11 a.m. on October 8, 1969, when he left his family to go hunting but did not return as darkness fell. As it grew darker, the snow began to fall heavily, and one and a half feet fell in the twenty-four hours following his disappearance.

Around sixty people participated in the search and rescue after the family contacted the Deschutes County sheriff. Helicopters were dispatched, and tracks were seen near a creek called Soda Creek at an altitude of 7,100 meters, considerably higher than Sparks Lake at 5,400 meters. The extensive search, however, did not turn up any signs of Winters or his equipment.

Near Soda Creek, near where the footsteps had been seen on the aerial search, Dr. Jack Crosby, a doctor on a hiking holiday in the area, discovered some items the following summer. As a result of Crosby's report to the sheriff, a search of the area was conducted.

The only things found in the vicinity after a three-day, detailed investigation by the sheriff's department were Robert's deer rifle and his clothes, plus one boot, one glove, and one pair of glasses.

Blood was not found on the clothes, nor were any remains found in the area. There was no evidence that the clothes had been shredded by an animal as part of an attack; instead, it looked like they had been removed carefully.

A detailed search of the scene failed to find a single bone despite the efforts of Mel Newhouse and Norman Thrasher, who were doing the investigation at the scene. The case remains unsolved.

ALISSA MARIE MCCRANN – MULTNOMAH FALLS

· · ·

ON SATURDAY, December 19, 2015, Alissa Marie McCrann, thirty-seven, from Portland, Oregon, disappeared while on a run near Multnomah Falls in the Columbia Gorge. Portland, Oregon, is about thirty minutes away from the wilderness attraction. Five years after her car was discovered and a large search was carried out, she remains missing.

The plan was for Alissa to run near Multnomah Falls. She left her Portland home in the Powellhurst-Gilbert neighborhood and drove to Franklin Ridge Loop trail in her Mazda CX-7 in order to go running.

In the Columbia River Gorge, east of Troutdale between Corbett and Dodson, Multnomah Falls is a waterfall located on Multnomah Creek.

The Franklin Ridge Loop hike is a worthwhile option for hikers who wish to combine the well-known waterfalls along Multnomah and Oneonta Creek with some peaceful solitude. It is also a smooth transition to the more strenuous hikes in this area.

In addition to living with her Korean parents, she also had a thirteen-year-old son. It was not known at the time if she suffered from any mental or physical health problems.

When Alissa failed to show up for work at Sunshine Dairy on Monday, December 21, the authorities were notified that she was missing.

On the nineteenth of December, her cell phone was used for the last time at around 10 a.m. to make a Facebook post. However, after that, all subsequent calls to her phone went directly to voicemail. It is estimated that the phone last pinged on Cascade Ave in Tigard, approximately forty-five minutes away from the falls.

Alissa's 2011 Mazda CX7 was discovered parked in Multnomah Falls' parking lot on December 22.

Around 3 p.m. on that Saturday afternoon, a couple walking near Multnomah Falls reported seeing a woman they believed to be Alissa. While she was wearing running clothes and shoes, she did not have any food or water with her, and she did not wear gear suitable for cold weather. In an apparent bid to remain warm, Alissa had run off down the trail when the couple said they had advised her to head back to her car.

One hundred searchers scoured 150 miles of trails in the gorge, focusing on Franklin Ridge, but no trace of the missing person has been found. In addition, there was over a foot of fresh snow at the higher elevations, which severely hampered access to the gorge. Sniffer dogs were deployed, but failed to detect any scent. Pilots flew over the area, but did not see McCrann anywhere.

Weather conditions caused the search to be suspended on Thursday, December 24, 2015. Before suspending search efforts, Portland Police Bureau's missing persons unit and a wilderness doctor from OHSU Hospital consulted with the sheriff's office.

One of Alissa's friends, Eric Ledecky, described Alissa as an upbeat, friendly person. "She'd do anything for you. She's the first one at your party. During birthdays, she gets you things. She'd help others out without asking for things in return. She's a good person. Everyone should have a friend like her."

On Saturday, January 23, 2016, the search for Alissa began again, which police then described as having moved from a search to a recovery mission. Some sixty volunteers participated, but no results were found. After the weekend search was over, the Facebook page dedicated to finding her posted an update:

"Even though we did not find her, it felt wonderful to know the community has not forgotten Alissa. Such an amazing outpouring of love and support. Again, all my love and respect goes out to the teams that helped orchestrate this latest search. They had a lot of manpower above the falls today and hopefully, the next search is the one that brings her home. We really miss her."

No trace of Alissa has been found five years after she disappeared. The timing of her running in December at such a late hour when dark would soon fall is weird, especially for an experienced runner in Oregon. Was hypothermia the cause of her running off trail and seeking shelter, which made it harder to find her body? Did she plan to intentionally disappear despite her thirteen-year-old son? She was not known to be suffering from any financial problems or mental disorders, however, so these are likely not to blame. This strange disappearance remains a mystery.

ROY LOREN STEPHENS – WILLAMETTE NATIONAL FOREST

ROY STEPHENS, forty-eight, a father of three, was last seen near Highway 58, near the town of Crescent, Oregon, in the evening hours. On November 25, 2005, his gray, 1991 Ford Taurus wagon was discovered off Highway 58, at Waldo Lake access road, in the Willamette National Forest.

Forest Service Road 5897 connects Oregon Route 58 to Waldo Lake, which stands at an elevation of 5,414 feet above sea level. There are eighteen miles between it and Oakridge, and the forest road leads to the lake for twelve miles.

In November of 2005, Roy picked up his paycheck and left his job at Odell Lake Lodge. Later, he called his wife, Marilyn Lightner, to ask if she would like to go drink and eat at a local tavern in Crescent City with him. She declined his offer because she was feeling unwell, and he went out and met up with his friends instead.

In the evening, he called her once again around 11 p.m. to let her know he loved her and that he was headed home. Those were the last words she said to him and the last time he was ever heard from.

On November 18, 2005, after waiting two days for Roy to return home, his wife reported him missing. Usually, he was a little late getting home and would call to say he would be back within a few hours, but this was out of character for Roy. However, he had never left the house overnight, and definitely not for twenty-four hours at a time.

When Roy didn't show up, Roy's wife and son searched the area near Odell Lake Lodge, hoping to find him. She reached out to neighbors and friends for support since she had just undergone triple bypass surgery. Since November 16, 2005, he has not been seen. According to friends, Roy left the tavern and was going to visit another friend before heading home.

Over a month after Roy had disappeared, on Thanksgiving Day, November 24, 2005, hikers walking up Waldo Lake Road saw a car and reported it to the police as abandoned.

The next day, the car was identified as Roy's, and it was within ten to fifteen miles of his home. It was in an opposite direction than where he was going to his friend's house.

The most bizarre and concerning part was that Roy left his wallet and paycheck in the car. In addition, there was a puddle of vomit lying next to the car.

Law enforcement agencies from Lane County, Klamath County, and the Willamette National Forest were involved in the case. The reason behind this is that Roy lived in Klamath County, yet his car was found in Lane County and also in the Willamette National Forest. After Roy vanished, cadaver dogs were not sent into the area for months. Not only did this hinder the search, but only four hours of searching were even conducted. He was

NATIONAL PARK MYSTERIES AND DISAPPEARANCES   19

clearly a low priority for search and rescue for some reason.

According to Krista Dolby, Roy's daughter, "... they didn't even do any forensic testing of his car. They looked in it for evidence, like his wallet and his paycheck were on the front seat, and apparently, the hiker reported that there had been vomit right by the car, but that's it. Then they arranged for the car to be towed back to my mom's house."

Since Roy disappeared from Waldo Lake fifteen years ago, no trace of him has been found. Although it was strange that his wallet and paycheck were left in the car, foul play does seem likely. Why didn't the assailants steal his belongings if he was attacked or murdered? It would seem likely that Roy would take his wallet if he wanted to disappear.

It is possible that he was drunk, got disoriented, stopped on the road, vomited, and then wandered off and got lost in the woods or was attacked by local wildlife.

There were rumors that there was some sort of conflict between Roy and the two men he was going to see. Local talk was that Roy was hiding something from those two men when he was last seen, but his community chose to remain very close-knit and closed-mouthed regarding the ordeal.

Law enforcement told the family that they wouldn't be able to go up the mountain because of safety concerns. The local community did not offer or volunteer to assist with the search for Roy. Why was Roy disliked by the community? Unless someone talks, we will never know.

DERRICK ENGEBRETSON – WINEMA NATIONAL FOREST

SOMETIME IN THE afternoon on December 5, 1998, Derrick Engebretson, his father Robert, and his grandfather Bob, sixty-four, set out for a densely wooded mountainside above Upper Klamath Lake, about thirty miles north of Klamath Falls. They planned to find a Christmas tree for the holiday season. Derrick was never seen again.

Because of his love of the outdoors, Derrick was known as "Bear Boy" at the age of eight. A week after he was born, his mother had carried him on a bear hunt in a pack. In his youth, he hunted with his father and picked mushrooms with his mother's father. On several of his mushroom expeditions, he had visited Pelican Butte.

East of the Cascade Range in south-central Oregon lies Upper Klamath Lake, a large, shallow freshwater lake. Pelican Butte rises over 3,800 feet above the shore of Crater Lake and is a steep-sided dormant shield volcano located 28 miles (45 km) south of the crater.

The Engebretson family did not plan to go Christmas tree hunting that year in the woods. Although Robert looked forward to a family Christmas tree hunt every year, it was his wife, Lori, who convinced him to use an artificial tree that year.

Lori wanted to keep the mess to a minimum, but when

NATIONAL PARK MYSTERIES AND DISAPPEARANCES   21

a disabled neighbor asked for a tree, Robert went into the woods.

Bob remembers telling his father that since it was already after 2 p.m., it would be dark around 4 p.m. since it was late in the year as he was driving along Westside Road in his red Toyota pickup. On his way to Rocky Point Resort, Bob pulled into a turnout at Milepost 12. The three of them climbed up an embankment into a pine forest after Robert helped Derrick get into his blue snow-suit. Derrick walked behind Robert, who told him to stay with his grandfather.

Derrick nagged his grandfather that he wanted to catch up with his father as he chopped at small trees with his hatchet. At some point, the grandfather relented, and the boy headed off in search of his father.

With the darkness closing in, Robert and Bob met up. "Where is Derrick?" Robert recalls asking. Bob replied, "I thought he was with you."

"He was with you!"

Despite the steady falling of heavy, wet snow, Robert turned back up the hill. He called out to Derrick, but no response came.

Robert flagged down Fred Heins, a motorist driving along the road at 4:13 p.m., and requested he dial 911 so that authorities could be notified. In the resort two miles away from the area where Derrick vanished, Heins made the call.

Over the course of two weeks, hundreds of people

searched through several feet of snow, using snowmobiles and dogs to search for Derrick.

Lori slept in a donated camper van at the turnout, hoping Derrick would see the bonfire and come to her. She thought she saw Derrick waving and smiling at her when she was delirious from lack of sleep. This was not the case.

Derrick's tracks were found by Robert and other members of the family in the newly fallen snow in the hours immediately following his disappearance. Derrick had lain down in a clearing near the road to make a snow angel, and his boot prints were spotted near the spot where Robert had last seen him.

There had been a snowplow that came by, and the tracks leading away from the angel were obliterated. There were no tracks leading toward the woods from the angel. A small area of the trees near the road was damaged by Derrick's hatchet cuts. The father was confident that his son did not reenter the woods. Early in the evening, five to eight inches of snow had fallen on Rocky Point.

A candy wrapper was found, and a makeshift lean-to shelter was found, made from branches, but it was unclear whether these items belonged to Derrick. Derrick's family believed that he had made his way to the road and was probably picked up by a stranger. This explanation was dismissed by the sheriff.

Bob discovered a hole in the ice in the lake and a child's footprint on the bank during the search. The next day, divers searched the area again, and additional searches were carried out during the spring thaw. However, nothing was found.

Lori and Robert were informed by Klamath County authorities that their son was likely dead eight days after Derrick disappeared.

During the next seven days, Robert, Lori, and about a hundred volunteers stayed on the mountain. Speculation intensified that Derrick had been kidnapped. When subzero temperatures forced the Engebretsons to end their search on December 18, 1998, Robert drove straight from his graveyard shift at work to the mountain to meet Lori every weekend for the next two years. The searched areas were marked on a map.

It was widely believed that authorities were too slow to arrive at the scene the night Derrick disappeared, which led to criticism of the search and rescue effort. The search did not begin until nearly five hours after the first 911 call, because the coordinator was reluctant to interrupt a Christmas dinner at Mollie's restaurant for the annual awards dinner of the Klamath County Search and Rescue team before he was certain a rescue was needed.

Despite passing polygraphs, Robert and Bob were suspected of murdering Derrick or having been negligent in some way. Despite his father's insistence, Robert couldn't speak to him. The blame for not finding Derrick went to him, but the blame for losing him went to Bob. Engebretson was too overwhelmed with guilt to even think of talking about it. Robert was on leave from work for several weeks. Derrick's family spent thousands of dollars looking for him, paying for psychics and a boat to search Klamath Lake. They eventually went bankrupt.

The authorities claimed Derrick wandered off into the woods and died, and his remains had been scattered by animals. However, the Engebretson family never really believed that, especially since no remains or torn clothing had been found. There was a witness who said he'd seen a man and a boy struggling on a highway nearby.

Then, in 1999, graffiti was scrawled on a rest-area bathroom wall near Burns stating that Derrick had been killed and buried. It was ruled a hoax by the FBI. A boy named Derrick who was found in Texas under unusual circumstances looked a lot like the Engebretsons' son, but was actually a different person. After several days of waiting for confirmation, a bone discovered in Pelican Butte in 2000 was identified as being from a deer.

In late 2001, the family mailbox received a hand-written letter. It read, "I know who took your son." On July 11, 2000, Frank J. Milligan, a thirty-one-year-old state youth authority worker, approached a ten-year-old boy at a Dallas park and offered him $100 to mow his lawn. In Milligan's car, the man asked the boy, "Do you want to live or die?" Milligan bound the boy's hands with duct tape and then forced him to walk down a dirt road and sexually assaulted him. Milligan choked the boy and slammed his face into the dirt so hard that he blacked out. He then cut the boy's throat and left him for dead. Despite the odds, the boy woke up covered in blood and got to a road, where a passing motorist stopped to help him. During the attack,

Milligan was out on bail from the Clatsop County Jail, accused of sexually assaulting an eleven-year-old boy in 1997. He ultimately pleaded guilty in both cases after being tracked down by the police. In a letter to police and the Engebretsons, Milligan's cellmate admitted that Milligan had abducted and killed Derrick. The letter arrived at the Engebretson home in late 2001.

A detective from the Oregon State Police who investigated the Dallas case confronted Milligan. Derrick Milligan confessed to killing him and agreed to lead investigators to his body.

The FBI used ground-penetrating radar to scan for Derrick's bones at Silver Falls State Park southeast of Salem, where Lori and Robert drove for five hours. There were no results after several days of searching.

An assistant district attorney told the Engebretsons that Milligan had agreed to plead guilty to killing Derrick if they spared him the death penalty. However, after Milligan was presented with the paperwork a few days later, he refused to sign it.

If the boy fell in the lake, his hatchet was likely to be in the water. It could indicate that the boy had died in the inlet if there was a hatchet in the sediment. Jeff Preece, a diver from Portland, spent several hours working his way through the shallow water using a metal detector designed for use underwater. An oil filter and a metal road sign were among the metal objects he found. However, he did not find a hatchet.

Was Derrick Miller abducted by Frank J. Milligan or

another pedophile, as the sheriff believed, or did he die from a cold or an animal attack? Is there another reason why Derrick Miller died that fateful and sad day in December 1998? The case is certainly mysterious.

GERREN KIRK – MOUNT HOOD NATIONAL FOREST

GERREN KIRK, thirty-one, took a lot of solo trips into the woods as a knowledgeable and experienced outdoorsman. On December 3, 2014, he left home to hike in the Mount Hood National Forest, and he planned to return on December 6. On this occasion, however, he did not leave any details with his family members.

His sister, Whitney Kirk Altman, reported Kirk missing on Sunday, December 7, but the search was delayed until Monday, December 8, since search and rescue crews couldn't be dispatched until the vehicle was located to determine a starting point.

Originally from Milwaukie, Oregon, Kirk attended Portland Public Schools' Vocational Village High School. For many years he worked as an admissions representative at the University of Phoenix in Arizona. As soon as he returned to Portland, he enrolled at Portland Community College to study business. After transferring credits to National University, he completed his first term of online courses. Upon completing his bachelor's degree, he planned to pursue a master's degree.

During his marriage to Kristin, Kirk was happy, but this soon ended, and the couple divorced after several years and shared joint custody of their daughter, Gabriella, who is five years old.

In the early morning of Monday, December 8, a family member found Gerren's gold Pontiac Grand Am parked in the parking lot of Frog Lake Campground, off US 26, focusing the search in heavily wooded areas near the campsite.

In addition to this, police were also able to locate his cell phone east of Frog Lake, heading southwest, after pinging it. In that case, he would have driven from Clackamas County into Wasco County, so the search was shifted to the Wasco County Sheriff's Office rather than the Clackamas County Sheriff's Office.

The search for the missing person took place near Frog and Twin Lakes, which lasted for around nine days and was coordinated by the Wasco County Sheriff's Office with the assistance of approximately 170 volunteers. Also participating in the search were sniffer dogs and infrared-detecting surveillance aircraft. It was mostly damp on the mountain over the period of the search, with temperatures slightly above freezing, and snow levels unusually low for December on the mountain.

Search and rescue groups participating in the search for Kirk included Multnomah County Search and Rescue, Pacific Northwest Search and Rescue, Lake County

Search and Rescue, Clatsop County Sheriff's Office, Clackamas County Sheriff's Search and Rescue, Wallowa County Sheriff's Search and Rescue, Klickitat County Sheriff's Office, Mountain Wave Emergency Communications, Salvation Army, Trauma Intervention Program, Zigzag, Welches and Sandy, Bud's Towing of Oregon City, the Milwaukie Presbyterian Church, and volunteers from several businesses in Government Camp.

Gerren was not found despite the efforts of the search teams. The fact that the cell phone was pinging in the direction of Clear Lake from the area south of Frog Lake was strange, but search efforts seemed to be focused on the vicinity to the northeast, in the area of Twin Lakes, which is unusual unless the media reported the location incorrectly.

Brian and Annette Kirk continue to keep Gerren's memory alive to this day by maintaining the Facebook page In Loving Memory Of Gerren Kirk.

THOMAS BRANCH MCADAMS – COLUMBIA RIVER GORGE

THOMAS "TOM" Branch McAdams, aged sixty-seven, went missing on Friday, September 23, 2016. He was headed for a hike near Horsetail Falls, in the Columbia River Gorge area, when he was last seen.

A report of his disappearance came in on September 26. His vehicle was found at the trailhead to Horsetail Falls in the Columbia Gorge parking lot on that day.

The Horsetail Falls are part of the Columbia River Gorge in Oregon. The waterfall is located right next to the Historic Columbia River Highway, so it is easily accessible. It resembles a horse's tail because of its shape and the rounded rockface over which it flows. The creek has two waterfalls. There is a footpath that leads to Upper Horsetail Falls, also known as Ponytail Falls.

Originally from Hartford, Connecticut, Tom was born on November 20, 1948. Tom and his three younger siblings were raised in Bloomfield, Connecticut, after his parents moved there shortly after Tom was born. Summers were spent learning how to sail and eating lobster on the coast of Maine as a child. Throughout his life, Maine has been a special place for Tom.

From 1967 to 1971, he studied at Kenyon College, majoring in religion. Despite not being religious, Tom disagreed with the war and the draft.

Tom drove out to Portland from his hometown in a VW van around the mid-1970s, then began studying nursing at Oregon Health and Sciences University in 1979, completing it in 1982. Tom began working at the Oregon Burn Center at Legacy Emanuel Hospital in 1978, where he spent the next thirty-eight years as a burn nurse. In January 2016, Tom retired from the Burn Unit.

Tom was active, healthy and loved the outdoors even when he was in his sixties. An avid skier, both downhill and cross-country, he also enjoyed sailing and canoeing. But hiking was his favorite pastime. Since moving to Portland, he has climbed Mount Hood, Mount Adams, Mount St. Helens, South Sister, and Mount Katahdin in Maine, and hiked the trails of the Columbia Gorge numerous times.

His wife, Cynthia, and daughters, Brittany and Alice, were his closest friends. With gray hair, green eyes, bushy eyebrows, and a mustache, he weighed 165 pounds and stood five feet eleven inches tall.

Several of Tom's recent signs of memory impairment and some personal issues were reported by the Portland Police Department after he went missing. Additionally, he didn't bring any hiking gear, which concerned Portland Mountain Rescue spokesperson Mark Morford. He said, "We're searching the waterfalls, looking around the base of the falls, looking in the pools, but there have been no clues. We always worry when a hiker is out that doesn't have the stuff to survive the night. We really encourage hikers going out to have the minimum gear to get through the night."

To help search the area around the falls, Morford's group sent nine searchers divided into four teams. Officials were optimistic because temperatures in the 60s would be able to help McAdams survive.

David Jenkins was hiking in the area at the time of the disappearance. He remarked, "It's beautiful and they've got well-developed trails here. I hike by myself sometimes and I've thought a lot about what if I have some trouble?"

In the hours between midnight and 2 a.m., dogs were

sent in to search for scents. On the first day of the search, search and rescue crews headed to the area at first light after the plane got a "credible" hit in the Nesmith Trail area, but no sign of Tom was found. Around 150 people searched over two hundred miles of trails in the Columbia River Gorge to find him, but without success.

Upon hearing of new information, the authorities announced that they would resume the search when credible new leads were found. However, these credible new leads never materialized.

Since Tom disappeared in 2016, no trace of him or his belongings has been found. The fact that he was experiencing some personal problems was a factor, but he seemed to have been a happy family man with two daughters. As he had not taken any equipment with him, it was clear that he was planning to hike for only a few hours. However, something unexpected happened.

As of yet, the mystery behind his disappearance remains unknown.

DAMING XU – THREE SISTERS WILDERNESS

IN THE LATE 1980S, Daming Xu, age sixty-three, came to the United States from China and became a professor of mathematics at the University of Oregon. His wife, Shixiu, and he enjoyed taking day hikes in Oregon's wilderness areas. Both were very fit for their ages.

Daming hiked up Olallie Mountain on November 4, 2007, in the Three Sisters Wilderness. He has never been seen again.

On November 15, one half of William L. Sullivan's trail book, *100 Hikes in the Oregon Cascades*, was discovered in the woods, which includes the Olallie Mount hike on page 154. Daming had left the other half in his car. Apart from that, there were no further clues found.

Olallie Mountain lies in the Willamette National Forest and is one of many smaller mountains that make up the Old Cascades, which were once ancient volcanoes before a shift in the fault zone moved the tall and snow-covered Young Cascades up to British Columbia.

An autumn trip into the Cascades was made perfect by a beautiful, sunny day with blue skies. A white shirt and a light leather jacket were Daming's only clothes for a day hike, but he did not have a backpack with him.

Stephanie and Paul Niedermeyer, who were also on a hiking trip, met him near the summit around 1:30 p.m. According to them, he did not spend much time at the summit before descending quickly.

Upon reaching the trailhead parking lot, the couple saw a white Chevrolet Impala that was semi-recently manufactured parked there. Their surprise was heightened when they saw it since the hiker (Xu) they had encountered on the summit should have been back by now—unless he had decided to go to the Olallie Meadows on the return trip, as the trail split. According to them, it was only logical to assume it belonged to another hiker on the French Pete Trail.

By the time the sun had set and darkness was falling, there was still no sign of the car's owner, and the couple became concerned. They pondered, "It's not like this easy hike had any challenges. Maybe he was just taking his time; it wasn't all that late yet."

However, a few days later, the Niedermeyers' fears would prove hauntingly true.

His wife reported him missing on the afternoon of November 5 after Daming failed to show up at home.

On November 6, his car was found near Terwilliger Hot Springs, with his cell phone, water, and heavier clothing inside. Several key pieces of a survival kit were also found inside.

His hike was not known to the authorities, except that it generally took place near Cougar Dam. Therefore, search and rescue were focused on an area that included Olallie Mountain, south of the McKenzie Bridge, Cougar Reservoir, and the Three Sisters Wilderness areas.

There were more than sixty mountain rescuers involved, including officials from Deschutes County Sheriff's Office, Eugene Police and Portland, Corvallis, Lincoln, Linn, and Lincoln Counties. Additionally, a UH-60 Black Hawk helicopter equipped with infrared FLIR was deployed.

The park rangers thought Daming must have taken the wrong trail at the junction and ended up at Olallie

Meadows rather than the parking lot. Still, he had to notice the difference in the trail, and that there was no meadow at the top. There was plenty of time to turn around after a mile of walking to the meadows.

It was thought that his tracks were near Bear Flat on the Olallie Meadows Trail, but sniffer dogs lost the tracks at this point.

The weather worsened later in the week following Xu's disappearance, with temperatures dropping and rain and snow falling. In the early days of November, Daming was extremely vulnerable without proper winter clothing.

According to the sheriff in charge of the search, the weather posed the greatest challenge to the lost man. On November 8, temperatures in the search area dropped below freezing overnight after being mild up to that point. A light jacket would not allow him to stay out overnight in these conditions, even though he was a fit and capable hiker.

Newspapers reported that the snow level would drop below the 4,700-foot level overnight due to rain and fog on November 10. It was expected that some accumulation would be present in parts of the search area that were higher than that.

Friends and volunteers continued to search Monday, November 12 despite the official search being called off due to bad weather. Nineteen agencies, dozens of volunteers, and over five thousand man-hours of searching were used to cover between fifty and one hundred square miles of thick forest.

NATIONAL PARK MYSTERIES AND DISAPPEARANCES   35

Sullivan's trail book, up to page 157, including the Olallie Mount hike on page 154, was found on November 15. Half was found in his automobile. If Xu had a map with him, how did he get so lost?

On the mountain's south side, the trail book was found in a very rugged area of the French Pete Creek drainage. Originally, Daming was believed to have followed the trail down to Bear Flat, then headed down French Pete Creek, where there was no trail. Due to the endless fallen trees, rocks, and steep terrain, French Pete Creek is extremely steep and hazardous, full of rocks, foliage, and trees. If he were still alive at this point, he would have either taken the French Pete Creek Trail back to Pat Saddle or down to Aufderheide Road 19.

In the following year, forty-five volunteers searched for the remains of Xu's body for four hundred hours without finding anything. Daming's wife, Shixiu, said the hardest part was that she had no remains nor a body to return to the family.

The death of Daming was a tragic one. For some reason, despite a beautiful sunny day and a good map, he seems to have gotten disoriented and wandered in the wrong direction. The weather turned bad shortly after he went missing, which was regrettable. It is likely that his remains will not be found, given the thick, inaccessible forest surrounding the French Pete Creek drainage, where his guidebook was found. Did he simply succumb to hypothermia, or was there something more sinister at play? The wilderness is not something you should take for granted even if you're an experienced hiker. The most obvious mistake Daming made on this day hike was taking no equipment with him.

A man named Jake Dutton disappeared from the same area five years later while on a solo hike. Apparently, this is not the best place to hike on your own.

COREY FAY – BADGER CREEK WILDERNESS

A STUDENT at Beaverton's Jesuit High School, Corey Fay was seventeen years old. It was 23 November 1991 when he agreed to go elk hunting with a friend of his dad's, Mark Maupin, and possibly his son, west of Tygh Valley, on the edge of Badger Creek Wilderness. On that particular day, Corey's father, the owner of Northwest Investment Cars, decided not to accompany them.

A year later, his remains were found in an area with waist-deep snow, ten miles away from the vehicle where he disappeared that day. So what happened to Corey when he was in the Badger Creek Wilderness area?

Due to his training in outdoor survival techniques and experience as a hunter, Corey knew what to do in an emergency environment. A compass, emergency solar blanket, food, rifle, and ammunition, as well as a backpack made up the remainder of this trip's equipment.

After arriving at the Wilderness around 6:30 p.m.,

the three men split up and arranged to meet back at the car within an hour. Apparently, the group was captured on CCTV as they went through a McDonald's drive-thru in Hood River around 6 a.m. or so. Could it be that the six o'clock reporting was incorrect and it was actually six o'clock in the morning? At that time of year, the sun sets around 4:40 p.m., so hunting that late would be unusual. Hunting after dark may actually be illegal in some states.

Hunting was difficult due to the cold weather. Maupin later told investigators that the area is well known for its presence of elk, yet they did not see any on that particular day. There was no sign of Corey in the vehicle as they returned. After searching the area for Corey and finding no sign of him, the group called the Wasco County Sheriff's Office and reported him missing.

About 250 searchers from the Rocky Mountain Search and Rescue based in Salt Lake City were involved in the rescue efforts, including helicopters, horsemen, hikers, and seven of the best-trained search dogs in the world. The team searched for ten days and ten square miles without finding any signs of Fay.

Although the official search ended on December 1, 1991, many volunteers continued searching for several weeks afterward. When the sheriff's office did not know what to do, the FBI was called in. Normally, the FBI wouldn't be called in for a case of disappearance, so there was likely foul play involved here.

Around ten miles from where Corey left the other

members of the group to go hunting, two hunters found Corey's backpack and rifle nearly a year later.

A mile away from these other items, on the same ridge at 6,500 feet, Corey's jacket was found following a more thorough search of the surrounding area. One tooth and small bone fragments were found a quarter mile from his backpack.

The most surprising finding was the absence of pants, boots, or socks. The grid searches of the ridgeline across a distance of one and a quarter miles failed to find any large bones normally associated with skeletons, such as ribs.

Corey would have been covered in snow up to his waist for over five miles at the time of the discovery, according to the sheriff. In an article published in the Eugene *Register* on September 18, 1992, it was reported: "Authorities know the snow was deep there because a helicopter had spotted tracks during an intensive search for Fay last November.

"The tracks turned out to be animals but the snow was almost waist deep, and that was a good three miles from where the items were discovered yesterday." The article later explains that searchers didn't believe Fay could have gone as far as he did and that it was odd he was going uphill when he should have been going downhill.

It has been verified by the sheriff's helicopter crews that, during November 1991, Corey's tracks were seen along a ridgeline at a point three thousand feet higher and ten miles from where he should have been hunting with waist-deep snow.

Because the terrain was rough and the area was not a common hunting ground for elk, neither the group nor the searchers saw an elk in this area if they were hunting there.

Due to the peculiar circumstances and evidence, this is a very unusual case. Some of the theories considered include the following:

An accidental shooting or foul play? According to the press, Cory may have been accidentally shot by another hunter or someone in the group and buried somewhere nearby. Perhaps someone shot him, dragged him away, and then returned after being ten miles away to drop off a backpack, gun, and tooth. Some accounts state that a lie detector test was to be administered to the youngest of the hunting group. After discovering the backpack, gun, and tooth, this line of inquiry was abandoned.

Was he injured before the hunt? There are reports that a surveillance tape shows another man driving Corey's pickup truck with what appears to be an animal or corpse in the back. Although McDonald's CCTV footage suggests this wasn't the case, authorities never investigated this lead fully. There's a wild theory that Corey's dad set him up on the hunting trip, and it was all his doing.

Hypothermia? How long did Cory survive? There was a possibility that one searcher found an old fire in a campsite, but the discovery wasn't confirmed. Since there were so many searches, it seems unlikely that he survived long after he first went missing. If Cory fell down in the snow and fell unconscious, he may have succumbed to the cold. Where's the point in walking through heavy snow so far from where the car is located? After becoming disoriented and walking uphill into a snowy area, Corey Fay's mother believes he may have died of hypothermia.

Suicide? Corey Fay suffered through a difficult week at school, according to a school friend named Steve Lopez. Some of the older cool kids disliked him after he attended a party. Due to this, he was feeling down before the hunt, and he explained that he had been feeling down recently. Could he have been contemplating suicide or going missing? As Steve said, "But we searched from there, we searched for days, we had hundreds of people searching. We had helicopters with night vision. There was no way that if Corey was alive that he was not going to be found, we would have found him. He would have fought to stay alive."

A mountain lion attack? Something attacking, killing, and dragging a seventeen-year-old with his rifle, backpack, and other gear any distance that would equate to his being ten miles and 3,000 feet above sea level does not seem likely. As a result of an animal attack, shreds of clothing, tissues, and blood would have been left behind but were never discovered.

Yet another mysterious death in the wilderness.

JAMES JACOB "JAKE" DUTTON – THREE SISTERS WILDERNESS, OREGON

. . .

ON JUNE 15, 2012, James Jacob "Jake" Dutton hiked the French Pete Trail in the Three Sisters Wilderness of Oregon. He never came back.

In the end, he was reported missing, but a search didn't begin for nearly six weeks since he failed to leave any sort of itinerary with friends or family. Due to his lack of employment and being single, the missing person report was also delayed.

About a hundred feet off the French Pete Trail, a hiker found Jake's remains on August 24, 2016. But what happened to him in June 2012?

Jake was thirty-two years old, lived in Eugene, Oregon, and had served in the US Coast Guard. Physical therapy was his field of study for alternative pain-relief methods.

Also, he was a seasoned hiker and camper, and he loved to spend time out in nature.

Douglas firs and western red cedars surround the French Pete Trail and drainage. The terrain is generally rugged and dangerous with many rocks and steep slopes.

French Pete Creek is only 4,823 feet away, and the trail itself ascends about 1,000 feet. The Three Sisters Wilderness has an average temperature of 21 degrees centigrade (70 degrees F) and a low of 5 degrees centigrade (41 degrees F) in June.

Jake was last seen at his apartment on June 3, and on Friday, June 15, he completed a form requesting a permit from the Forest Service, in which he outlined when he intended to begin and end his hike. According to him, he had planned to return on June 18.

Later in June, after a family reunion in Seaside, he planned to take his thirteen-year-old nephew camping, and it is believed that he went to the trail to scout out campsites for the future excursion.

Cynthia Boucher, Jake's mother, became concerned about him in mid-June when she tried to reach him on his cell phone to remind him about his older brother Christopher's birthday.

Jake was supposed to give his nephew a ride to the Portland International Airport on June 28 but failed to show up. On July 9, Jake's brother went to Jake's apartment and discovered that there was no sign of him, so he notified the authorities.

The report, which included the pickup's license plate number and description, allowed the US Forest Service to track it down. A blue 1998 Nissan Frontier pickup truck was found on July 30, 2012, near McKenzie Pass on forest road 19 near the trailhead for French Pete, off Aufderheide Memorial Drive near McKenzie Pass. Oddly enough, Jake's backpack, inflatable boat, and hiking boots were found in his apartment and not in the truck.

The French Pete area of the forest did not have cellular coverage, so even though Jake had his phone, he was unable to use it.

He had not returned from his hike, and his pickup was still at the trailhead. His family was disappointed that Forest Service officials did not use the permit to figure this out.

On July 31 and August 5, law enforcement personnel,

volunteers and search and rescue dogs participated in two searches. Jake was not found during either search.

Similar to Jake Dutton, Daming Xu also disappeared in the same area after ascending Mount Olallie on November 4, 2007. While his guidebook was found near the French Pete Creek, none of his belongings or body were found. You can read about Daming Xu elsewhere in this book.

In the Three Sisters Wilderness, a hiker discovered Jake's skeleton on August 24, 2016. About four miles from the trailhead, the remains were located. Almost four years had passed since he disappeared.

In the steep, heavily forested area, Jake's remains were found next to his backpack and two bear spray cans. While Jake was still wearing pants, his torso had been stripped completely. Authorities suspect that Jake died of hypothermia, as there was no evidence of foul play, such as trauma or gunshot wounds to the body.

A hike in the wilderness alone is never a good idea, and this is especially true in the French Pete Trail area of Oregon if you have not left an itinerary behind with friends or family members. Be careful out there.

ROBERT MICHAEL BOBO – ROGUE RIVER–SISKIYOU NATIONAL FOREST

. . .

ON OCTOBER 28, 1998, ROBERT "BOB" Michael Bobo was camping in a heavily wooded area of the Rogue River National Forest near Prospect and Union Creek, Oregon. The area is west of Crater Lake National Park, where several mysterious disappearances have taken place.

Around 9 p.m. on October 2, 1998, hunters in the area saw a female dropping him off at his campsite in the Woodruff Meadows area near 700 Road. In Woodruff Meadow, he had been living alone for a few weeks. He was a part-time woodcutter.

Bob was nowhere to be found the following day when his friend came to pick him up. It appears that he had vanished from the campsite without a trace.

Oregon and California are home to the Rogue River–Siskiyou National Forest. 2004 saw the administrative unification of the formerly separate Rogue River and Siskiyou National Forests. Currently, the Rogue River–Siskiyou National Forest extends westward from the crest of the Cascade Range into the Siskiyou Mountains, spanning almost 1.8 million acres (7,300 km^2).

Bob's friend arrived at Woodruff Meadows to pick him up for the start of the hunting season on October 3, 1998, but could not locate him, even though he did not have his own vehicle.

Bob was reported missing to National Forest Rangers immediately.

Bob left his favorite black Pape Cat cap, two rifles, and all of his clothes and camping equipment behind, which worried his friends and family. He had no money to leave on his own since he was too familiar with the area to get lost.

In the area surrounding Bobo's campsite, numerous searches were undertaken, but no evidence was discovered. Although there were no indications of foul play, authorities do not believe Bob left of his own free will.

Robert Bobo was one of the three men from the Rogue Valley who disappeared into the area's forests around 1998.

The incident was investigated by Jackson County sheriff's deputies. "It's just suspicious. We don't know what happened," Detective Dan Hobbs said, suggesting that Bobo could have left the campsite and perhaps suffered a serious injury or medical emergency of some sort.

Robert's brother, Dennis, would go to the Prospect area at least once a month to search for skeletal remains, looking for clothing, fabrics, and bones, but never found anything. "We've played a million scenarios through our heads," Dennis says. "We're reasonably sure he's not going to show up."

Dennis believes that the fact that his baseball cap was left behind is sufficient proof that his brother was murdered. Dennis said, "When he woke up in the morning before he even went to the bathroom, he put his hat on." He was self-conscious of his receding hairline, so he never left the house without wearing a hat.

Furthermore, Dennis Bobo said his brother knew the terrain too well to become lost. If his brother had suffered some major medical problem, he doubts he would have wandered very far, and even if he wanted to leave, he was too poor.

When he was last seen alive, Bob scrounged dinner and drinks from friends in Prospect before hitching a ride to the campsite. That sounds like a person who was planning on going deer hunting in the morning, not leaving town, if they were that broke and dropped off at the campsite fourteen miles outside Prospect.

Dennis Bobo feared his brother had met foul play and complained to the Jackson County Sheriff's Department given the circumstances. "There's no evidence of foul play as they consider it, but put two and two together: Where is he if there's no foul play?"

Sheriff's Detective Dan Hobbs was quoted as saying this to Dennis' concern: "Good question. At this point we have nothing to indicate foul play, needless to say, it is suspicious in nature that he would up and disappear like that. Basically, we've done all we can do," he says. "I sympathize with the family, not knowing, but we're just grasping at straws here."

Despite taking a number of leads, Hobbs says none of them came to fruition. Prospect buzzed with rumors about Bob's disappearance, as he ran with what many considered a somewhat sketchy crowd.

It is highly suspect that Bob Bobo left all of his gear, including valuables like his firearms, at the camp. The night of October 1998, was he attacked in his camp by someone or something? To this day, Bobo's body is still missing, and no proof of an animal attack has been uncovered. This is yet another strange disappearance in Oregon, to which we may never know the answer.

ROBERT PERRY BISSELL – ROARING RIVER WILDERNESS AREA

FIFTY-SEVEN-YEAR-OLD ROBERT BISSELL OF PORTLAND, Oregon, left his home on July 12, 2010, to go camping in the Roaring River Wilderness Area near Rock Lakes above Estacada, Oregon, just to the southeast of Portland.

Bissell often hiked alone into remote areas to enjoy the solitude and fish in solitude as a backcountry backpacker.

Robert had filed a wilderness-use permit with the Forest Service, saying he planned to return on July 16. Since then, he has not been seen.

At Trailhead 700 near Rock Lakes, Robert parked his car, a white 1989 Nissan Sentra with Oregon license plates, and hiked off Trail 512 to set up his tent. In spite of leaving his sleeping bag and gear at the campsite, he took only his fishing rod and tackle with him, as if he intended to be gone only for a day or two.

On July 19 and July 24, when his brother went to the campsite and found no sign of him, he reported him missing.

Clackamas County Sheriff Search and Rescue began

an extensive eight-day search early on Sunday, July 25, 2010. Search areas that were part of the large-scale search included the Roaring River Wilderness, the Rock Lakes Basin, and surrounding trails, as well as lakes, including Serene Lake, Shining Lake, and Shell Rock Lake.

Several other campers reported to rangers meeting Robert in the Roaring River Wilderness Area near Estacada at the beginning of his trip. In a note that he left behind, Bissell outlined when he would head into the wilderness area and when he would return.

As his rod and fishing tackle were gone, authorities believe he set up camp, then hiked out to fish in Rock Lakes Basin. In the surrounding lakes, there were plenty of trout to catch.

There were flyers posted in campgrounds, trailheads, ranger stations, and all over the nearby town of Estacada, asking for information.

It is possible Bissell was injured seriously while hiking through the Rock Lakes Basin in the Mount Hood National Forest, according to Sergeant James Rhodes of the Clackamas County Search and Rescue Unit. In spite of cold temperatures in the area at the time of Robert's disappearance, Rhodes and his team were confident in their ability to find him. "It gets chilly at night, but it's not the kind of weather that pushes people into hypothermia." The area had no cell phone service, however.

The search involved hundreds of volunteers, including sixty to seventy professional searchers, two fixed-wing aircraft, a helicopter, rescue dogs, horseback patrols, ATVs, and 4x4 units, as well as searchers on foot.

Over a dozen lakes were searched by helicopter, while surveillance planes flew grid patterns over the area. Teams of sniffer dogs from Yamhill County and Clark County, Washington, were called in, along with the Air Force Reserve 304th Rescue Squadron and Pacific Northwest Search and Rescue, who scoured the terrain for any sign of the missing man.

Generally, searchers deployed in six-member teams. Following standard search-and-rescue protocol, they moved into new areas while shouting Robert's name and blowing whistles. However, they received no response.

When the search ended on August 3, there were no signs of Bissell's whereabouts in the Mount Hood National Forest. In fact, three of the search horses threw their shoes because the terrain is so rough.

A number of items were found during the search that they believed Bissell might have left behind. However, all the items they brought to base camp each time did not belong to Robert, according to his brother, Michael Bissell. Robert had been spotted by other campers, who told investigators they spoke with him when he set up his camp.

Robert's clothing and fishing gear have not been found. It was as if Robert has simply disappeared without a trace.

RONALD ALLEN OHM – WILLAMETTE NATIONAL FOREST

ON THURSDAY, August 9, 2012, Ronald "Ron" Allen Ohm, fifty-two, was hiking with two friends near Russell Lake in the Mount Jefferson Wilderness area in the Willamette National Forest when he mysteriously went missing.

While the others set up camp downstream, he decided to stay on a ridge above the lake for a while and take pictures. The rest of the group headed down, leaving Ron behind.

Having been an experienced hiker, Ron was familiar with the region and was equipped with a blue and red backpack, tent, sleeping bag, and provisions that would last for several days. Due to a medical condition he was suffering from at the time, he took four days' supply of tablets with him, since he had to take daily medication.

The evidence does not point to Ron Ohm ever having made it back to the lake from the ridge near Russell Lake in the Mount Jefferson Wilderness.

Despite the fact that an extensive search effort has taken place over several years, no remains nor equipment have been found despite the fact that a great deal of effort has been put into searching.

Having departed from the Breitenbush Lake campground trailhead, the group planned to spend the next few days at Russell Lake, which is located northwest of Portland.

There was no sign of Ron at camp that night on Thursday, August 9, 2012. On Friday afternoon, his friends went looking for him, then hiked out on Saturday evening to report him missing.

Several other agencies, as well as Portland Mountain Rescue, were involved in the six-day search, in addition to the Marion County Sheriff's Office. Search officials from Linn, Benton, Deschutes, Lane, and Polk Counties and Portland Mountain Rescue were also involved. Several search crews searched the area between Russell, Scout, and Bays Lakes. In addition to searching for Ohm on foot, they looked for him on horses, in SUVs, and on ATVs.

Throughout the search area, helicopters from the Oregon Army National Guard and Cessna 182 aircraft from the Civil Air Patrol used numerous hours of flight time, flying over the area for hours on end, but they were unable to locate any trace of Ron. During the search, fliers were posted at trailheads and along the Pacific Crest Trail in order to inform hikers of the location of the missing person.

Over two hundred searchers searched three hundred square miles of the Willamette National Forest north of Mount Jefferson for over 3,500 hours. Smoke hampered efforts, as did the approaching "Waterfall 2" forest fire, which was moving west from Warm Springs.

Around Russell Lake, there are many ridges and valleys covered in forest and some snow. It can get very hot during the day. The search area ranged in elevation from 5,000 to 7,500 feet above sea level.

MCSO Search & Rescue volunteers from Team 18, along with personnel on horseback and in Jeeps, returned to the area a year after Ron's disappearance in the hopes of finding his remains. The search involved fifty-four people, who spent two nights in the wilderness to maximize search time. The trailheads of the Breitenbush and the White Water trailheads were searched along the Pacific Crest Trail. Although 1,135 man-hours of searching were spent on this second search, no evidence was found.

It has never been possible to find any remains, clothing, or equipment connected to Ron Ohm. It's another case of someone going missing in Oregon and taking pictures in the wilderness who mysteriously disappears despite a large search. Would Ron have walked away and taken his own life, having told his friends that he planned to take pictures? Were there bears or mountain lions in the area? Yet no clothing, cameras, or equipment was left behind. Sadly, the truth may never be known.

THE COWDEN FAMILY – COPPER

THE COWDEN FAMILY went camping in the Siskiyou Mountains near Carberry Creek, Copper, Oregon, over Labor Day weekend. The party consisted of Richard (twenty-eight), Belinda (twenty-two), David (five), and Melissa (five months), and the family dog, Droopy, went with them. As Applegate Lake was created in 1980, Copper was flooded and no longer exists.

Their bodies were discovered in a bizarre scene seven months later, in April 1975, around seven miles (11 km) from their campsite. Considered by many to be one of the most mysterious murder cases in American history, the case remains unsolved.

Richard Cowden drove logging trucks in the Cowden family's hometown of White City, Oregon. In their 1956 Ford pickup truck, the Cowdens drove to the campsite.

Campouts were not planned for Labor Day weekend 1974 for the Cowden family, though they enjoyed going camping. It was Richard's intention to haul a load of gravel for his driveway and complete the job over the weekend. Due to a problem with the truck, the family decided to go up to the mountains for a trip away.

Northwestern California and southwestern Oregon in the United States are home to the Siskiyou Mountains, a coastal subrange of the Klamath Mountains. An arc of these mountains runs along the north side of the Klamath River (about one hundred miles north of Crescent City, California) into Josephine and Jackson Counties, Oregon. Mountains separate the Klamath River basin to the south and the Rogue River basin to the north.

Rogue River–Siskiyou and Klamath National Forests contain most of the range. Along part of the range, the Pacific Crest Trail winds.

In the early morning hours of Sunday, September 1, 1974, Richard and David went to the Copper General Store to purchase milk on foot. After leaving the store, they returned to their campsite. This was the last time anyone saw any members of the Cowden family alive.

A short distance from the campground, Belinda's mother was expecting the family to stop for dinner on their way home. She went over to the campsite to see what was going on when they failed to appear.

When she arrived, she found the Cowden family gone and their truck parked beside a picnic table with the keys on the table. It was clear that Belinda's purse was on the table, and a plastic dishpan full of cold water lay on the ground. In addition to the diaper bag and camp stove, there was also a half-finished carton of milk, which matched the one purchased earlier. Unexpectedly and alarmingly, Richard's expensive wristwatch and wallet containing cash were found lying on the ground. An open pack of cigarettes, the brand Belinda smoked, was also found. Despite the truck appearing untouched, all of their clothes were inside, and only the bathing suits were missing.

In about an hour's time, Belinda's mother notified the authorities, which resulted in the arrival of the sheriff, troopers, and the Oregon State Police District 3 Office. The officers searched the area until it got so dark that nothing could be seen.

Lieutenant Mark Kezar, who led the case, later stated that the investigation had been "delayed for maybe a day," due to the lack of evidence of any violence occurring at the

NATIONAL PARK MYSTERIES AND DISAPPEARANCES   55

campsite. As a state trooper, Officer Erickson described the tableau: "That camp was spooky; even the milk was still on the table."

Droopy, the Cowden's pet basset hound, was found scratching at the Copper General Store's front door the next morning, September 2. However, his owners were nowhere to be found.

Hundreds of volunteers, including state and local police, Scouts, the Forest Service, and the Oregon National Guard, took part in the search for the Cowden family, one of the largest in Oregon history. Infrared imaging was carried out by helicopters and planes equipped with infrared imaging to search twenty-five miles of roads and trails surrounding the campsite. Even after this very extensive search, no signs were found other than the dog. A search of the area was officially suspended on September 7, but family members and friends spent many weekends and vacations searching.

Richard's family had little debt, no late payments, and made more than enough money to sustain them. It was unlikely that they would have voluntarily vanished. The cash-filled wallet, expensive watch, etc. were left behind, so it certainly did not seem like a robbery. Despite the creek being so nearby, no bodies were found, so accidental drowning was ruled out. Where were the Cowdens? Police were puzzled.

Seven months after the family vanished, two gold prospectors were hiking through the woods near Carberry Creek on April 12, 1975. Around seven miles from where the Cowdens camped, they made the grisly and horrifying discovery of the decomposing body of an adult male tied to a tree on a steep hillside. A child, an infant, and an adult female were found dead in a small cave nearby. The cave entrance was carefully covered with rocks so the bodies could be hidden and disguised. Dental records were used to positively identify the bodies.

According to autopsies, both Belinda and five-year-old David were killed by .22-caliber gunshot wounds, and baby Melissa had suffered severe head trauma, which caused her death. Due to the advanced state of decomposition, the cause of death for Richard Cowden could not be determined by medical authorities.

Investigators searched the area for a gun or other weapon because they suspected Richard could have killed his own family. The weapon used by Richard to murder his family members and to commit suicide would still exist if he was indeed responsible. But no weapon or gun was ever discovered.

Afterward, Lieutenant Mark Kezar stated that "The whole nature of the thing smacks of a weirdo," explaining that the police know a lot that they were not comfortable discussing.

Richard and David returned to the camp after going to the store, and the family went swimming in adjacent Carberry Creek in the afternoon, according to the authorities. Shortly afterward, probably before noon, the family was abducted at gunpoint by a stranger. Apparently, they were driven some distance away, forced up the steep slope where they were found, and at least three of them were shot, Kezar speculated.

On September 1, a family from Los Angeles, California, had arrived at the campground at 5 p.m., and while walking in the park that evening, they saw two men and a woman parking in a pickup truck nearby. The family would later state, "They acted like they were waiting for us to leave, and frankly, they made us nervous, so we moved on."

Because of the location of Belinda and the children's bodies inside the cave, Lieutenant Kezar suspected a local resident who knew the area and was aware of the cave's location was responsible. Upon discovering the family's remains, someone in Grants Pass who had volunteered in the search told police that he had searched the cave where Belinda and the children's bodies were found in September 1974, and they hadn't been there. Police confirmed the story by having the man take them to the cave where the bodies were found; it was the same cave he had searched.

An interview with former Oregon State Police detective Richard Davis about his involvement with the Cowden case was conducted in August 2020.

The OSP, Jackson County Sheriff's Office, and Central Point Police conducted months-long searches to find the suspect, which Davis describes as "chasing their tails." "He had two recruits come in and you go up on the Applegate and look for buzzards because buzzards will lead us to the body. This was in January. Buzzards are migratory birds, there hadn't been one in the Rogue Valley, Applegate Valley since early November," Davis explained.

Several early suspects were eliminated quickly, he said. After months of no new leads, officers lost hope in the case. "We got some of the strangest most bizarre calls, tips where they were and what they were doing... they were seen in Seattle, they were seen in San Francisco. They weren't," he said.

Davis says two campers from Washington made a gruesome discovery seven months after he took over as lead detective. "They started up a little game trail from the level camp spot up the hill... and there was a skull," Davis said. "Right then, I mobilized everyone I can get. I need help. I'm one man, I can't search the forest. I need help," he complained.

The skull belonging to Richard Cowden was recovered roughly seven miles from the camping site, says Davis. Richard Cowden was bound to a tree.

Richard's wife's, son's, and baby's bodies were hidden behind some rocks in a small cave on the hillside about a hundred feet away. "The boy had been shot by that .22 rifle. I don't remember how Belinda was killed. The baby had had its head bashed in by blunt force trauma," Davis recalled.

He says they bagged everything, including the soil the bodies had been lying on. However, after being exposed to the elements for over half a year, any signs were rare.

"During the actual search and recovery for bones and stuff, the men became kind of giddy. But once we got back into the vehicles, it became very somber. Reality sets in. My god, what have I been doing? How could I have been giddy up there on the hillside when this family's been murdered, brutally murdered?" he said.

"One bullet, belonging to a rifle manufactured by Marlin, was all that remained," Davis said. "We're looking for anybody that had purchased that weapon that could have fired that shot. A weapon that could have fired that shot," Davis said.

The murders were linked to Dwain Lee Little, but he was never charged. He had been released from Salem's Oregon State Penitentiary on May 24, 1974, three months before the Cowdens vanished. A fifteen-year-old girl named Orla Fay Fipps had been raped and murdered by Little on November 2, 1964. In determining that Little had been in Copper over Labor Day weekend, the police determined that he had been there when the Cowden family was killed.

After Little's girlfriend informed the authorities that she saw him with a .22-caliber gun during Christmas 1974, his parole was revoked on January 12, 1975. Having been paroled a second time on April 26, 1977, Little picked up a pregnant twenty-three-year-old named Margie Hunter, whose car had broken down near Portland, Oregon, on June 2, 1980. Despite sexual assault and a beating, she was able to survive. In that case, Little's charge and conviction for attempted homicide resulted in his being sentenced to three consecutive life sentences in prison. The accused murderer refused to discuss any of the killings he was accused of and never cooperated with mental health treatment.

Due to the similarity of their truck to that described by the Los Angeles family at the campground, police believed Little and his parents were inside the truck reported by the family. Both Little and his parents denied knowing anything about the Cowdens' disappearance. However, a miner who owned a cabin nearby claimed that Little and his parents signed a guest book he kept for visitors when they stopped in on September 2, 1974.

One of Little's cellmates, Floyd Forsberg, would later claim that Little confessed to the murders of the Cowdens.

Following the discovery of the bodies a few months later, Richard Cowden's father committed suicide, but was never charged with anything.

Over four decades later, the truth about the Cowdens' murders remains a mystery. Dwain Little or someone else? There was certainly foul play, but who was it? All we know for certain is that an egregious crime took place in the wilderness of Oregon. Someone literally got away with murder.

TWO
HAUNTED OREGON

Rhododendron Village
East Autumn Lane
Rhododendron, OR

In this region, also called Laurel Hill, there were the most dangers on the Barlow Road, the overland route of the Oregon Trail. Ghost stories are plentiful today, as deaths were frequent in the 1840s.

Pioneers traveling the Oregon Trail camped at this site during the 1800s. Lighting that turns on and off by itself, strange sounds, doors slamming and opening, and orbs floating in photos—to name a few things people have reported. While doing restorations on the property, several graves were found, which may explain the hauntings.

Columbia Gorge Hotel
4000 Westcliff Dr.
Hood River, OR
(541) 386-5566
https://www.columbiagorgehotel.com/

THE STRANGE HAPPENINGS at this hotel include the smell of cigar smoke said to emanate from a former resident who died here many years ago, furniture barricaded inside rooms when there are no guests, and several different ghostly visitors. A man wearing a white frock coat and top hat has been seen, as well as a woman who jumped from a hotel balcony wearing white. Room 330 is haunted by a female ghost, and the ground floor used to have a pool where a child ghost has been observed.

***

Hood River Hotel
102 Oak St.
Hood River, OR
(541) 386-1900

A FORMER OWNER is believed to haunt this hotel, which is the oldest inn in town. The reception desk has been reported to make phantom phone calls when unattended, and doors to some rooms open and close on their own. In addition, guests have reported hearing disembodied voices, knocks on the walls and door, and footsteps coming from empty hallways.

It offers forty-one rooms and suites, is listed on the National Register of Historic Places, and has been the subject of many paranormal investigations.

Multnomah County Poor Farm (Edgefield Hotel)
2126 SW Halsey St.
Troutdale, OR
(503) 669-8610
https://www.mcmenamins.com/edgefield/discover/
history

THE MODERN INCARNATION of the Poor Farm, the McMenamins Edgefield, is the hotel you need to search under if you wish to stay at this truly haunted hotel. At one time, this site was an asylum for mentally challenged, aged, and disabled people. The premises are rumored to still be haunted by the spirits of many of the residents who died here. A wide range of ghost sightings and paranormal events have been reported, ranging from human ghosts to dog ghosts. Children have been heard crying in a wing that used to be an infirmary, a woman has been sighted in several rooms, and some have been woken up by a ghost dog shoving its cold snout into their faces in the middle of the night.

Heceta Head Lighthouse
725 Summer St, Florence, OR 97439
https://www.hecetalighthouse.com/

ON OREGON'S COAST, thirteen miles north of Florence, stands the Heceta Head Light.

The lighthouse is fifty-six feet high and shines a light that can be seen over twenty nautical miles out to sea. This makes it the most powerful lighthouse along the coast of Oregon.

Here are some ghosts residing in the lighthouse.

The region was explored by the Spanish explorer Bruno de Heceta in the late eighteenth century. The lighthouse bears his name. The area was once inhabited by the Siuslaw Indians, who hunted sea lions and collected seabird eggs there. Their legend relates to the cliffs as well, a stone wall built by the Animal People. They used the stone wall to trick the Grizzly Bear brothers into falling to their deaths.

Erected in 1892, the lighthouse became operational two years later. In addition to the lighthouse, there were houses for the head lightkeeper, two assistant lightkeepers, and their families. A barn and oil storage buildings were also present on the site. 1963 saw the automation of their systems, and 1978 saw its addition to the National Register of Historic Places. The facility closed for extensive renovations in 2011.

The main haunting at Heceta Head isn't the lighthouse itself, but the houses that surround it. This ghost is known as Rue, and it is believed that it is connected to the grave of a baby that is found on the site. The baby's cause of death is unknown, but the grave is real, and most locals believe that Rue lost her child there.

In another version of the story, Rue's daughter either perished off the cliffs or drowned in the pond where they lived. The little girl was buried on the grounds of the lighthouse, and her mother committed suicide in grief.

Strange incidents have been reported at this house since at least the 1950s. There are reports of strange noises and objects moving on their own, as well as the occasional scream of a woman. Though this is speculation, it is believed this is Rue's scream of horror when she found that her child had died.

Rue is an active ghost who makes strange noises as well as screaming and rattling dishes in the kitchen cabinets and flickering lights on calm nights when there is no explanation for it. Even lockable doors are left wide open by her.

The Grey Lady is another ghost who haunts Heceta Head. The Grey Lady haunting Heceta Head may or may not be the same spirit as Rue, the grieving mother.

A mist hovers over the house where the Grey Lady appears. In a story from the 1970s when the property was undergoing renovation, she appears in a more solid form as well. In the attic, she came face-to-face with a painter who fled and refused to return.

During an accident, he broke the attic window after being reassigned outside. However, he was unwilling to clean up the broken glass after replacing the window. At night, the owners heard scraping noises in the attic, and in the morning, all the glass was neatly piled up.

It has been reported that there have been over a hundred ghost sightings in Heceta Head. In fact, *Life* magazine even did an article about the case.

Shanghai Tunnels – Portland Underground
120 NW 3rd Ave.
Portland, OR
(503) 622-4798

SHANGHAI'S TUNNELS rank as one of the most haunted places on earth, which should come as no surprise to anyone. Travelers say they feel goosebumps in the tunnels as if someone is watching them. A lot of people say they have seen an Asian man walking past them. The spirit is known as "Sam" and turns off the lights in bar basements, as per the explorers. Additionally, Sam enjoys moving things about in the tunnels when explorers pass by. One tour guide reported hearing a voice repeatedly calling out the name "Sam."

His guests were terrified after hearing the voice. He

NATIONAL PARK MYSTERIES AND DISAPPEARANCES   67

knew that it was not one of them because his entire group was behind him. "It was the scariest thing I've ever done!" he said. When no one else is around, some have perceived quick movements of shadows and felt ghostly fingers on their shoulders. The majority of tunnel tourists say that Sam is a good ghost, and they enjoy being around him.

Another type of tunnel spirit is a trickster, who just enjoys having fun. You may find them tugging gently on your hair or pulling at your shirttail. There was a guest who reported feeling a small tug on her shirt before she fell. The experience was not painful, but she said it will never be forgotten.

Despite the fact that most ghosts in Shanghai tunnels are friendly, it is better to remain cautious. A person or something may have felt unwelcome or like it was watching them. Prior to being thrown to the ground, one man recalled hearing childlike whistling. In an effort to see who knocked him down, he turned around. Looking behind him with his flashlight, he could not see anyone. It was the man's last trip to the Shanghai Tunnels. The tunnels have some reports of ghostly activity, but for the most part, these experiences are not that frightening.

Bring your own water and stay with your group at all times, as you will experience complete darkness! It may seem scary at first, but you will definitely enjoy the tour. Definitely take a trip through the Shanghai Tunnels at least once if you are interested in taking part or interacting with spirits.

You never know who or what lurks down there in the dark in the tunnels... you need to keep your wits about you.

Fort Stevens State Park
Near Astoria, Oregon
https://stateparks.oregon.gov/index.cfm?do=park.profile&
parkId=129

FORT STEVENS STANDS as a testament to America's relentless spirit, a relic of the wars that built it. As the defender of the Great River of the West, Fort Stevens still holds a special place in military history despite the absence of bloodshed. For those who find themselves in Portland and want a break from the hipsters, Fort Stevens is a good choice. There are times when the ghostly soldiers out there are lonely, with only the moss creeping over their encampment and the wind blowing through their trees.

There have been reports of paranormal activity in the area from hikers and other tourists. Experts believe people's spirits are not always tethered to the exact spot where they died but can be drawn to places that hold emotional meaning for them. However, some people believe that a person's soul, trapped between worlds for whatever reason, is free to roam wherever it wishes. Fort Stevens seems to attract restless spirits for whatever reason.

Hot Lake Hotel/The Lodge at Hot Lake
66172 Highway 203 La Grande, Oregon
(541) 226-3944
https://hotlakelodge.com/

WITH ITS THERAPEUTIC waters and medical innovation, this resort attracted visitors from around the world at the turn of the last century, with the Mayo brothers (from the Mayo Clinic) among its most notable guests. The hotel went out of business after a fire destroyed half of the building in 1934. Afterward, what was left of the original building was then used as a retirement home, a school for nursing students, and even an insane asylum before later being abandoned.

In the fifteen years following the building's abandonment, various stories circulated about hauntings that occurred there, some of which were connected to its troubled past. There have been rumors of the building being haunted by old vacationers, a nurse who drowned after getting scalded in a lake, and a gardener who killed himself on the property when it was an asylum.

There was a piano on the third floor of the hotel that once belonged to Robert E. Lee's wife. The piano is said to have played by itself more than a few times over the years. Donna Pattée, onetime owner of the hospital, and caretaker Richard Owens reported hearing screaming and crying from the hospital's surgery room, as well as rocking chairs moving on their own. When the property was a restaurant in the 1970s, Pattée and her husband lived on the second floor of the building, where a lot of activity seemed to be centered. As a result of the property's alleged hauntings, it was featured on an ABC television series in 2001 called *The Scariest Places on Earth.*

Geiser Grand Hotel
1996 Main St, Baker City, OR 97814
(541) 523-1889
http://www.geisergrand.com/

THE GEISER GRAND Hotel is one of Oregon's most historic hotels. Gold Rushers called it the "Queen of the Mines" when it first opened in 1889. It hosted many high-class events in the early twentieth century. Oregon's wealthy patrons eventually moved on to other hotels after the hotel became a hospital during WWII. After the war, the hotel sat vacant for many years. In time, it was renovated to become the Geiser Grand Hotel. Most of the spirits in the hotel are friendly, say ghost hunters. The hotel's most famous ghost is called "Lady in Blue" since she always appears in a long, flowing blue gown to guests.

Multnomah Falls
Columbia River Gorge

THE MULTNOMAH FALLS holds the record for the tallest waterfall in Oregon. Visitors can get to the waterfall by hiking the trail that starts at the Multnomah Falls Lodge. As one of Oregon's oldest historical sites, the lodge dates back to 1925. Located near the trail's highest point, visitors can see an astounding waterfall. A Native American woman jumped off the falls to her death, say locals. During the winter months, hikers have reported seeing a woman's figure just beneath the water's surface.

PART 2

WASHINGTON

THREE

MYSTERIOUS DISAPPEARANCES

RICHARD R. LEE – WENATCHEE-OKANOGAN NATIONAL FOREST

AS OF SEPTEMBER 9, 2004, Richard Lee, forty-seven, of Hobart, King County, had gone hiking alone in Washington State's Wenatchee-Okanogan National Forest on a two-day trip. In the area of the Cascades, he planned to explore Colchuck Lake, an area familiar to him from hiking in the wilderness.

When Richard set out, the weather was perfect, but the terrain was rugged. During those two days, he used a cell phone to call his brother and let him know all was well. Then he disappeared.

Richard Lee failed to appear at his Hobart home on September 11. He was reported missing to authorities on

September 15 by his wife, who was initially unconcerned when he didn't return home on September 11.

Immediately, searchers began focusing their efforts on Lake Stuart, Colchuck Lake and Enchantment Lakes to the southwest of Leavenworth. The search and rescue effort was complicated by eight inches of snow that fell around the same time. Volunteers from King, Yakima and Kittitas Counties assisted the Chelan County Mountain Rescue crews with the use of three planes from the Department of Transportation.

In the end, the search teams found Richard's car off the trail, along with his campsite. To prevent bears from getting to his kit, his sleeping bag and food were kept in a tree. Unfortunately, nothing else has ever been found relating to Richard Lee. None of his remains, gear, or clothing have ever been found.

Lee's camp seemed "uncomfortable" to some searchers, but they didn't explain why.

KAREN SYKES – MOUNT RAINIER NATIONAL PARK

IN JUNE 2014, Karen Sykes, seventy, made the trek to Owyhigh Lakes in Mount Rainier National Park.

Karen hiked ahead of her partner once they reached snow level at an elevation of about 5,000 feet. She said she

NATIONAL PARK MYSTERIES AND DISAPPEARANCES   77

would walk a short distance up the trail, then return. However, she was never seen alive after that. What happened to her?

The hiking community in Northwest America was well acquainted with Karen Sykes. In addition to writing for online publications and newspapers, she was also a photographer and wrote a book describing hikes in western Washington. In addition, she authored a popular trail column and produced articles about Washington hikes for the *Seattle Times*, as well as co-authoring a second book about hikes in wildflower areas. Additionally, Karen wrote a blog called "Karen's Trails," where she shared hiking-related stories, photos, and trail reports.

Her close friend Lola Kemp said, "She is a trail guru," adding that she hiked twice a week and was a climber and scrambler.

As part of her research for an article she planned to write, Karen and her boyfriend hiked near or along the Owyhigh Lakes Trail on June 18, 2014.

Despite Mount Rainier's 14,410-foot height, she had adequate survival gear to camp overnight.

Karen took a faster pace than her hiking partner and vanished during the day.

According to Greg Johnston, a former outdoors writer for the *Seattle Post-Intelligencer*, Karen was a strong hiker who knew the mountain well. "She's the last person anyone would expect to get lost, particularly on Mount Rainier," said Johnston, who commissioned Sykes to write a weekly hiking column for the newspaper for more than a decade. "If anybody can survive it, it's her. She's really tough and really savvy."

The area was scoured by six ground crews, two dog teams, and two aircraft. After three days of searching, rescuers located a body in rocky, steep terrain in an area that was hard to access and not heavily used.

Karen had died from hypothermia, according to an autopsy by the Pierce County Medical Examiner's Office. It was 40 degrees Fahrenheit in the park when she was missing.

Karen's death was caused by heart disease as a secondary cause, but she didn't have any other injuries, so her death was ruled an accident. Although Karen's daughter and friends reported that she was healthy and fit despite the autopsy finding of heart disease.

In spite of the well-marked trail, Karen seemed to have become lost. In one moment, Karen was next to her boyfriend; in the next, she was lost. Whether Karen suffered from hypothermia, a heart attack, or something else spooked her is unknown.

ERIC LEWIS – MOUNT RAINIER NATIONAL PARK

ON THURSDAY, July 1, 2010, Eric Lewis, fifty-seven, of Duvall, Washington, went missing while mountain climbing on Mount Rainier. The climbing companions were left to pull up a coil by a butterfly knot after he had unclipped from the rope and disappeared. The search for Eric ended when only his pack was found in a snow cave after he vanished.

However, his body remains missing even now after ten years. Is it possible that Eric was spooked or killed by someone or something, or was it that his gear just failed? So far, no one has been able to fully or satisfactorily explain just what happened on Mount Rainier on that fateful day over ten years ago.

Located in Washington, Mount Rainier is 14,411 ft (4,392 m) tall and is about 59 miles (95 km) from Seattle and northeast of Portland, Oregon. It is also known as Tahoma Peak or Tacoma Peak.

Mount Rainier is a large active stratovolcano in the Cascade Range in the Pacific Northwest. It is the highest mountain in Washington and the Cascade Range. As a result of the high probability that Mount Rainier will erupt in the near future, it is one of the world's most dangerous volcanoes.

As the first access route to Rainier's summit, Gibraltar Ledges were used. Hazard Stevens and Philemon Beecher Van Trump successfully climbed this route in 1870, and it has become the "standard" route on the mountain for winter climbing.

This is the route Eric and his companions were climbing that day in 2010. As the three-man team ascended the Gibraltar Ledges route on Mount Rainier in high winds and low visibility, Eric became inexplicably separated from his two climbing companions.

On the Ledges route, Don Storm Jr., the climber in the lead, paused and was joined by Trevor Lane, the second climber on the rope. The rope had only a coil and a butterfly knot when they pulled it in at 13,900 feet as they awaited Eric's arrival. The men had glimpsed him on the rope just moments before and searched the slope below them immediately.

To make sure Eric had not skirted around them during the search below, the group headed to the summit ridge after thoroughly searching the area beneath. Upon not finding him at the summit ridge, they returned to Camp Muir, the high camp for climbers at 10,200 feet, and notified rangers of the incident. A search was immediately organized.

A Chinook helicopter flew above Nisqually Ice Fall and Gibraltar Chute, areas where Eric might have ended up. A team of climbers searched those areas. Late in the day of Eric's disappearance, Tom Payne and two mountain guides searched for him at the summit. More than forty people participated in the search the next day. Mountaineering guides from Rainier Mountaineering Inc., Alpine Ascents International, and Olympic Mountain Rescue volunteers conducted the ground search.

The search from the air was conducted by helicopter rangers aboard a military Chinook from Fort Lewis and a commercial helicopter from Northwest Helicopters.

Eric's backpack, climbing harness, and snow shovel

were found at 13,600 feet, as well as a small snow cave at 13,800 feet. There was no sleeping bag, tent, food, or even a down jacket in the gear Eric carried, which was very concerning. As such, he was ill-equipped to survive on the mountain.

Don Storm and Trevor Lan performed a thorough search for Erik and retraced their steps. At least that's what they claim. Could they have cut his rope deliberately, perhaps for unknown reasons?

Simon Yates cut his rope during an ascent of the west face of Siula Grande, which Joe Simpson wrote about in his book and later film *Touching the Void*, in 1985 while he was climbing the Huayhuash range in Peru. Simpson fell over the cliff in an accident while roped to Yates, who was forced to cut the rope to keep both climbers from falling. Simpson survived despite having broken bones and being unable to work after crawling out of a snow cave. His escape from death in the Andes was miraculous.

The ground was covered in snow, so it should have been easy to find Eric's footprints, but he didn't leave any besides those of his companions. There were no indications that he strayed from the group. The searchers found his climbing gear in an ice cave two hundred feet below where he disappeared.

Eric Lewis was never located on Mount Rainier despite this extensive search.

Questions remain to this day. What could have prompted him to cut himself from the rope? After sheltering in the ice cave, did he suffer from hypothermia and become confused and disoriented? Did something or someone scare him into cutting his rope out of pure, unbridled fear? Was he trying to commit suicide? Sadly, we will probably never know the truth.

SAM B. DUBAL – MOUNT RAINIER NATIONAL PARK

A THIRTY-THREE-YEAR-OLD MAN, Sam Dubal, left Friday, October 9, 2020, for a solo hike in Mount Rainier National Park and was due back the next day. On that day, he was spotted near Lake Mowich in the park, on the Mother Mountain Loop trail. When Sam did not return to his home on October 12, his family reported him missing.

In addition to his tent and sleeping bag, Sam also had rain and snow gear, a cell phone, and a solar-powered charger. He was well equipped for the overnight hike. He was also experienced in challenging conditions. Sam was not located despite an extensive search.

Mount Rainier is among North America's most dangerous mountains because of its potential for volcanic eruptions, but there have also been many hiking deaths on its icy slopes due to accidents, mishaps, foul play, and other causes.

Mount Rainier has a 14,411-foot summit and is an active stratovolcano in Washington's Cascade Range, about fifty-nine miles south-southeast of Seattle. It is part of Mount Rainier National Park. In the US state of Washington and the Cascade Range, Mount Rainier is the highest point. Due to the high likelihood of an imminent eruption, the mountain is considered one of the world's most dangerous volcanoes.

In addition to trips around the United States, Sam Dubal had trekked in the Himalayas as well. He earned his PhD in medical anthropology from UC Berkeley in 2018 after graduating from Stanford and attending medical school at Harvard. As an anthropologist, Sam enjoyed studying the human condition within past and current societies.

After completing the joint medical anthropology program, Dubal worked as a field researcher in Uganda, working on the Lord's Resistance Army, a militant Ugandan group known for war crimes. It led him later to write a book, *Against Humanity: Lessons from the Lord's Resistance Army,* that critiques the concept of humanity.

A professor of anthropology at the University of Washington since June 2020, he joined the department as an assistant professor. Professor James Pfeiffer, who teaches anthropology and global health at the University of Washington, said, "He was the kind of scholar and public intellectual we really need in the world right now. Having him as a member of the faculty was a huge honor for the university."

At the time of his disappearance, Sam Dubal weighed 155 pounds and stood five feet nine inches tall with black hair and a short black beard and was wearing a blue jacket.

Nine days of intense searching were conducted by Mount Rainier National Park Service search and rescue teams. Sam's car was found shortly after he was reported missing, and his water bottle was found several days later.

Dubal's whereabouts were searched on the ground and by air by the National Park Service and the US Air Force. The area searched ranged from 2,000 to 5,000 feet in elevation and included dense forests, rocky terrain, and subalpine meadows.

In good weather on October 17, a fifty-person search and rescue team searched the area, but the following day, poor weather limited the team to fewer searchers. A twenty-six-person search and rescue team searched the area where Dubal was believed to be hiking on October 20, but bad weather on October 21 and 22 limited their ability to search on the ground. As a result, the search was suspended, and Sam was presumed to be deceased.

The National Park Service (NPS) announced on October 22 that teams had resumed the search for Sam Dubal on the ground, following a request from the family. The family said a petition had been started on October 22, requesting that rescue teams continue searching for him for seventy-two additional hours.

The snow had covered much of this area by that time, and the temperature had fallen below freezing, even at lower elevations. One day after he set off, a storm washed out the crossing he was going to use to cross the Carbon River.

Mount Rainier National Park has logged a record number of sixty searches in 2020 alone, and several deaths have also been reported.

Sam remains missing despite these efforts.

SAMANTHA SAYERS – NORTH CASCADES MOUNTAINS

DURING A SOLO HIKE on the Vesper Peak trail in Washington's North Cascades mountains, Samantha "Sam" Sayers, twenty-eight, went missing on Wednesday, August 1, 2018.

Sam left on the trail around 8 a.m. and was due to report to her boyfriend, Kevin Dares, around 6 p.m. that evening. Kevin was at work that night, so he was unable to accompany Sam. When she didn't return, he decided to go to the trail around 8 p.m. when it was getting dark. She was reported missing the following morning around 1 a.m.

As of this writing, there has been no sign of her.

Vesper Peak Trail has been described by the Washington Trails Association as not for novice hikers, but for those looking to go beyond hiking into backcountry adventure, it's a good starting point. On this summit, stumbling is much less likely to result in serious consequences than on other summits along the Mountain Loop. According to some hikers, the Vesper Peak trail is "hard to follow," suggesting that Sayers may have strayed from the trail by accident.

At the time of her last sighting, Sam was dressed in gray hiking pants and a black sports bra. Due to alopecia, Sam has no hair on her head. A veteran hiker, she had previously explored the Vesper area.

As soon as she was reported missing, the Snohomish County Sheriff's Office conducted a search that was one of the longest and most ambitious rescue operations in recent years.

Sam's car was found parked along the Mountain Loop Highway in the Mount Baker–Snoqualmie National Forest, twenty-seven miles south of Darrington.

The Vesper area was searched by seventy searchers on foot, fourteen dog teams, and two helicopters without success. Sheriff's Marine Unit members and drone operators participated at one point. Additional volunteers from across the state spent thousands of hours looking for the missing woman and left bags containing dry socks, a poncho, energy bars, a compass, a flashlight, fire sticks, and lighters with a note that read, "Stay strong! We are looking for you."

Sheriff's deputies spoke to witnesses who saw Sam the day before she disappeared, but none saw her returning back down toward the trailhead.

She had lunch with an unidentified male before she disappeared, according to Kevin Dares, her boyfriend.

After he saw the news of Sam's disappearance, the unidentified person checked in with searchers to say that he'd had lunch at Vesper Peak at roughly 3 p.m. that day with Sam. In addition, he said he later saw her going down the west side of the mountain towards Spada Lake after they parted ways.

As of August 2, sheriff's office search and rescue teams have put in 357 hours of air operations, 105 hours of drone operations, 82 hours in the marine unit to assist the search teams in Spada Lake, 329 hours for search and rescue personnel, and thousands of volunteer hours.

On August 23, 2018, the official search for Sam was called off without finding any sign of her. Sergeant John Adams of the search and rescue unit stated, "We have exhausted all leads and tips. We've interviewed all witnesses who have come forward. We have checked and double-checked the possible routes we believe Sam could have taken. If there was a place we thought she could get to, we put people there to look for Sam, often putting our volunteers and personnel at great risk due to the rugged, remote, and dangerous terrain."

Using the $39,000 raised on a GoFundMe page, however, family members conducted the search with private helicopters, dog teams, and a professional tracker. Facebook members helped with tasks, including searching hours of drone video for signs, thanks to a group set up by the family.

No evidence whatsoever has been found regarding Sam's whereabouts despite the extensive searches.

JAMES THOMAS GRIFFIN – OLYMPIC NATIONAL PARK

PRIOR TO CHRISTMAS 2014, James Thomas Griffin, sixty, of Port Angeles, traveled to Washington State to hike at the Olympic National Park. Other hikers last saw him around 4 p.m. on December 22 at Olympic Hot Springs. When he failed to attend a Christmas Eve dinner with friends as planned on December 24, he was reported missing.

There was no sign of James on Christmas Day, even though his daypack had turned up. One month later, on January 25, 2015, James' body was found near the top of the trail, almost one thousand vertical feet above the ground. How could this have happened?

Retirement, singleness, and living alone were all aspects of James' life. As a frequent visitor to the park, he knew the trails very well, as he was an avid hiker. However, he was often affected by an old leg injury, so he sometimes made slow progress.

December 22 and 23 of 2014 saw rain and cold temperatures in the mid-thirties in Olympic National Park. This harsh weather may have added to James' difficulties with his injury during the hike.

The state Department of Emergency Management search dogs and their handlers helped ten rescuers from

NATIONAL PARK MYSTERIES AND DISAPPEARANCES   89

the park and Olympic Mountain Rescue. Bud, James' dog, also assisted in the search for him.

In the Olympic peninsula's Elwha Valley, about a half mile from the trailhead of the Boulder Creek hiking trail and fifty feet off the trail itself, James' daypack was found on Christmas Day. Besides his camera, stove, food, water, snacks, and fire-starters, the pack was leaning against a log, looking as though it had been removed. Besides the towel, a can of cola and a coffee mug, as well as an unopened bag of resealed freeze-dried food, were resting on top of the pack.

No signs of struggle could be seen in the area, and the camera contained a picture of a nearby waterfall.

The body of James, despite a weeklong search, was not discovered until Sunday, January 25, 2015, where it was found nearly one thousand vertical feet above the trail and about a third of a mile from where he disappeared.

The park officials stated Griffin appeared to have stepped off the trail to prepare a snack, but then became disoriented and was unable to find his way back. Olympic National Park spokesperson, Barb Maynes, said, "There is nothing to suggest anything other than someone who lost his location and couldn't find his backpack again, where he stepped off the trail and became lost and disoriented."

In response to the question of why he climbed the steep hill where his body was discovered, Maynes said: "If it's dark and you can't see anything, it's easier to walk uphill. You're more in control."

Dr. Eric Kiesel of Clallam County's forensic pathology department released an autopsy report that indicated

James suffered from hypothermia. According to James' brother Robert, the results were "really odd." He continued, "It's just one of those things that happened, and nobody will ever know what the reasons were for him going up the hill."

James Griffin's case is peculiar. Leaving his food and pack off the trail, why did he climb one thousand feet up a steep hillside? Could something or someone have scared James enough to cause him to drop his daypack and food and flee as fast as he could?

It would have been difficult for him to climb one thousand feet of steep slope in pitch black if he had an old leg injury, and why did he leave his car if he knew the area well? What was it that scared James in the Olympic National Park?

The investigators believe he simply got disoriented and then got lost in the dark on the way back to his car. This is despite the well-marked trail. His autopsy revealed no signs of intoxication. The Olympic National Park continues to be a place of mystery, and James' death is yet another for this area. In the end, all we have is conjecture as to what happened and another strange hiking death.

GILBERT MARK GILMAN – OLYMPIC NATIONAL PARK

· · ·

ON SATURDAY, June 24, 2006, Gilbert "Gil" Mark Gilman, forty-seven, went for a short walk in Washington's Olympic National Park but did not return.

Rather than go for a serious hike that day, he headed to the trailhead of the Staircase Rapid Loop Trail in the National Park to take some photographs. His clothing and footwear were light, and he was not carrying a backpack. A short conversation with Park Ranger Sanny Lustig followed Gilman's parking his car at Staircase Ranger Station, and that was his last sighting. An extensive search lasting ten days failed to find any trace of Gilman. Since his disappearance fifteen years ago, there have been no signs of his whereabouts.

Would Gil have planned to disappear and work as a covert agent for the US government? The question is: Did he succumb to something in the Olympic National Park, or was he murdered by a serial killer?

Gil stood five feet seven inches and weighed between 155 and 165 pounds with graying brown hair and brown eyes. On the day of the visit to the Olympic National Park, he was wearing a bright blue and green Hawaiian shirt, khaki pants or shorts, sandals, and prescription sunglasses.

Despite his toughness and intelligence, he had a friendly disposition. He was a former US Army paratrooper who had served in East Africa, Panama, and Israel. Two Bronze Stars were awarded to him for his service with the 82nd Airborne.

A graduate of the London School of Economics as well

as Union College in New York and Solvay Business School in Brussels, Gil holds a degree from each institution.

In the past, he has worked as an interrogator in Iraq and as a counterterrorism and counterintelligence analyst. Additionally, he spent a year as a contractor in Iraq and is fluent in Arabic, Russian, and Chinese.

Before coming to Washington State to manage the 2004 congressional campaign for Sandy Matheson, director of the state Department of Retirement Systems, Gilbert worked for the United Nations in New York. From April 2005, he served under Matheson as deputy director of the retirement systems department and advised her on national and local pension issues.

A park ranger, Sanny Lustig, noticed Gil on June 24, 2006, carrying a camera without a backpack. Sanny said, "I could actually hear the music playing in his car and went out to see what was going on and I had a brief conversation with him and asked him to turn down the music. I got the sense he was going for a hike."

Olympic National Park's Staircase area lies thirty minutes outside Hoodsport, in a lowland old-growth forest. Located here are a seasonal ranger station, a campground, and the trailhead for the North Fork Skokomish River Trail, a wonderful place for backpacking or for day hikers to begin the Staircase Rapids Loop.

This 2.1-mile loop trail winds through a canopy of Douglas fir, western hemlock and western red cedar trees, some three to four hundred years old.

Mossy trees and ferns line the trail as it follows the

North Fork Skokomish River. At its terminus is a large fallen cedar. The river is crossed by a suspension bridge, which offers views of the rapids. High water in 1998 destroyed the original bridge, which was rebuilt much higher to accommodate spring run-off in the area. The North Fork Skokomish River Trail leads to Flapjack Lakes after an approximately fifteen-mile round-trip hike.

On the day after Gil's hike, on Sunday, June 25, 2006, Sandy Matheson was to accompany him to a meeting in Spokane, Washington. Gilman's disappearance was reported to the authorities when he failed to meet Sandy as originally planned.

Several days after Gilbert Gilman went missing, the 2005 Ford Thunderbird Convertible he was last seen in by Sanny Lustig at the Staircase Ranger Station was found.

No trace of Gilbert was found in the North Fork Skokomish River, steep hills, dense forest, and nearby trails in the Staircase area during the ten-day search. The search team used sixty-two searchers on the ground along with a helicopter, a plane and tracking dogs. Having searched for ten days without success, the US Forest Service declared the official search as suspended.

"It's hard to imagine a person can just disappear," said his mother, Doris Gilman. "Nothing was ever found."

On August 27, 2015, Gil was declared legally dead. Washington state law presumes someone dead if they are missing for at least seven years without being heard from, with an absence that "is not satisfactorily explained after diligent search or inquiry."

His mother, Doris Gilman, filed a petition in June 2015 with the Thurston County Superior Court. With this, she became the official estate trustee and held the power to settle Gil's estate.

Being lost on the Staircase Loop Trail is uncommon since it is short and well marked, unless he got lost and continued on the North Fork Skokomish River Trail. A thorough search was conducted of the area.

There has been at least one previous incident of someone going missing after hiking along the Staircase trail. Two hikers were reported missing in the 1980s after they hiked in the Staircase area but were never found.

In a few television shows in the following years, some theories were presented about Gilbert's disappearance. KIRO-TV reported in 2008 that Gilman had been involved in top-secret military intelligence work and "led a mysterious life." Gilman's mother believes the former Army intelligence officer may have decided to become a spy for the United States government and disappeared as a result.

Serial killer Israel Keyes may have murdered Gilman, according to a 2014 episode of the Investigation Discovery series *Dark Minds* hosted by M. William Phelps.

As a prisoner in Anchorage in 2012, Keyes committed suicide. From 2001 to 2003, the avid hiker lived in Neah Bay, Washington, and he obtained "a few overnight backcountry permits," which allowed him to access the Olympic National Park at that time. Keyes competed in a marathon in Port Angeles around the same time that

Gilman went missing (he placed ninetieth in the race), according to author Molly Koneski.

From 2001 to 2012, Keyes is suspected of killing eleven people from Vermont to Washington. In Washington, he allegedly killed a couple and two individuals, then dumped them in lakes, including Lake Crescent near Port Angeles, which is 650 feet deep at its deepest point.

Keyes was arrested by the FBI at age thirty-four after admitting he had murdered an eighteen-year-old girl in Anchorage. The FBI said he sought many of his victims while hiking, camping, and in remote locations. It seems that he went around the United States on trips into the wilderness. It is believed that he sought out murder victims on these trips and disposed of them discreetly in order to avoid detection.

Based on evidence and reviews of unsolved homicides and missing persons cases, FBI Special Agent Kevin Donovan said Keyes was unlikely to be involved in Gilman's disappearance in March 2014. Although Keyes' involvement is not clear from Koneski's theory, it certainly is convincing.

JOHN DEVINE – OLYMPIC NATIONAL PARK

. . .

SEVENTY-THREE-YEAR-OLD JOHN DEVINE went camping and hiking at the Olympic National Park in Washington on Friday, September 6, 1997.

As an experienced hiker, he had planned to climb Mount Baldy, which rises 6,796 feet above Olympic National Forest. He planned to do so by using the extremely steep Maynard Burn Trail.

After the hike on September 7, he failed to return home as planned, and his family reported him missing to the police.

The search for John was cut short by a fatal helicopter crash while looking for him.

He lived in Sequim and was in excellent physical shape, even though one of his eyes was legally blind. He had hiked for long distances alone in the Olympics prior to this.

On the afternoon of September 7, he was last seen walking along Gray Wolf Ridge on the park's north side. In the Buckhorn Wilderness Area of Olympic National Forest, just outside the park's boundary, he had been camping since Friday night with a friend.

He had snack bars but no other food or gear.

At the five-thousand-foot level of Mount Baldy, twenty miles south of Port Angeles, a Bell 205A-1 rescue helicopter crashed, killing three people and injuring five others. Following takeoff from a mountainside, it fell. The pilot, Kevin Johnston, thirty-five, was a former Oregon flight instructor and left behind an eighteen-month-old daughter; plus Rita McMahon, fifty-two, a dog trainer who volunteered for rescue missions, and Taryn Hoover, thirty-one, a seasonal park employee were also killed.

Survivors Robert Feldmann, twenty-seven, of Mukilteo, and Cynthia Stern, twenty-four, of Port Angeles, escaped unharmed. Another passenger, Heidi Pedersen, thirty-two, of Port Angeles, was listed in stable condition at the Olympic Memorial Hospital in Port Angeles.

At the time of the crash, snow and cold had swept through the mountainous region.

The search for John continued into the night in the Mueller Creek area, but the dozen searchers were brought out well before dark. Jason Berry, twenty-three, who was serving his second year as a Park Service volunteer said, "It's steep and rugged... the bushes are super thick and it's tough to walk down the drainages."

Clallam County Sheriff's Office's Sergeant Don Kelly, who helped coordinate the search with members of the National Park Service, said: "If he was walking around up there, we would have found him by now. And if he had fallen down and hurt himself, he probably wouldn't be alive."

On September 13, 1997, the search was called off. The location of John Devine was never discovered. And so we are left with yet another bizarre disappearance from within Olympic National Park.

BRYCE HERDA – OLYMPIC NATIONAL PARK

. . .

ON APRIL 9, 1995, Bryce Herda, six, went missing while hiking with his family on Shi Shi Beach. The site is located southwest of the Makah Indian Reservation, close to Olympic National Park, not too far from Seattle.

Bryce was four and a half feet tall and weighed sixty pounds, was of medium build, and had brown eyes and light brown hair when he disappeared. He was Native American/Caucasian and had a medium complexion. The mole on his right temple was about one-eighth inch in diameter, and a one-inch vertical scar ran across the center of his forehead by the hairline.

Seeing that he could not walk up the trail, he agreed to meet them back at the beach. Bryce was last seen on the beach when his family left to walk up an adjacent trail. However, he was nowhere to be seen when they returned.

When the boy went missing, his grandfather was the chief of police, so resources were deployed quickly and in large numbers. Approximately thirty searchers, including Coast Guard helicopters, combed the area where he was last seen within forty-five minutes of his disappearance.

With specialized equipment, there were increasing numbers of ground and water crews searching all night for any signs of life. Dog teams and more crews joined the search the next day, and by the end of a week there had been thousands of people in the area, including US Air Force personnel and rock climbers. There were also people searching the coast and driving off-road. A week after the search started, agencies called it off, but Bryce's family is still searching. Some footprints were found, but they were inconsistent.

No trace of Bryce or his clothing has ever been found, leading the family to believe he had been abducted by a stranger. A homeless community was adjacent to the Ozette Trail. Despite police speculation that his body may have washed out to sea, it was never recovered.

How long was he left on the trail before his family's return, and why couldn't he follow them up the trail from the beach? Was Bryce kidnapped while on the trail?

The case remains open and unsolved as of this writing.

CHET E. HANSON – MOUNT RAINIER NATIONAL PARK

DURING THE SUMMER OF 2007, Chet Hanson, twenty-seven, lived in Wilkeson, Washington. Hanson was an avid nature and outdoor photographer.

Chet left for a photography excursion in Mount Rainier National Park in Washington at 6:30 a.m. on November 11, 1997. While he was leaving, his mother said goodbye, and he assured her that he would be back before dinner. The camera equipment he brought with him weighed about thirty-five pounds, including lenses and a tripod. His clothing consisted of shorts, a fleece top, and hiking boots.

He did not show up for dinner as planned that evening, but his parents were not too concerned since they believed he might be staying with friends. The Alaska Airways company called the parents at 2:30 p.m. to tell them he had not arrived at work as expected, and at this point he was reported missing.

His car was found at the trailhead of Deer Creek Falls in the park after a search was started by friends and family. Chet's disappearance was reported to the Wilkeson police and then to the park rangers. A set of negatives, a key chain containing a set of house keys, a glasses case, and some miscellaneous papers were found in the car. Photographs from the Tipsoo Lake area were on one negative and those from Highway 410 on the other.

Chet was an avid hiker who avoided the trails and walked cross-country where he was familiar with Mount Rainier's environment. Recently, he had been photographing lakes and waterfalls, which provided some valuable clues to the searchers as to where he might be found or at least where he might have been heading. Willard Olson and his girlfriend reported seeing someone matching Chet's description on Shriner Peak on November 11 at around midday.

Neither Chet nor his camera equipment was ever found in spite of an extensive search with sniffer dogs, cadaver dogs, and at least a hundred searchers.

No trace of him was ever found.

ALEXANDER "ALEX" PISCH – NORTH CASCADES NATIONAL PARK

ALEXANDER PISCH, thirty-five, was last seen on Thursday, October 8, 2020, near Colonial Creek Campground and Diablo Lake in Whatcom County, North Cascades National Park. A campground is located off Highway 20 in Washington State, about an hour east of Rockport. At the site, his easel was mysteriously abandoned while he was painting a landscape.

Alex is a Californian from Discovery Bay. He is six feet one inch tall and weighs 160 pounds.

He had set up the easel for painting near his white Toyota Corolla parked along Highway 20.

An employee of the park service noticed Pisch's car and easel in the same spot on Saturday, October 3.

A search began for Alex in Diablo Lake and Colonial Creek Campground on Sunday, October 4. In the following week, approximately twenty people searched for Pisch. As of October 2021, there has been no sign of Pisch.

Fifty thousand acres make up North Cascades National Park in Washington State. A portion of it is located in the north and another in the south, and it is divided by the Skagit River.

Among its highlights are the rugged peaks of the North Cascades Range, the largest glacial system in the contiguous United States, the headwaters of numerous waterways, and the most diverse flora of all American national parks.

When European American explorers arrived, the region was inhabited by the Skagit tribes, who were descendants of Paleo-Indians of the area. At the beginning of the nineteenth century, there were fur trappers in the region, and several US and British companies vied for control of the lucrative fur trade in the area.

Several dams were constructed in the Skagit River valley for generating hydroelectric power in the 1920s, the first significant human impact in the region. On October 2, 1968, environmentalists created the North Cascades National Park to preserve the remaining wilderness.

To this day, there is only speculation as to what happened to Alex. Was he snatched by a mountain lion? There was no blood, torn clothing, no signs of a struggle. Could he have met with foul play or otherwise been abducted? As of 2021, there are no answers.

There have been several disappearances in the area of North Cascades National Park. In Spanish, *diablo* means devil, and the area seems to be the center of strange and dark occurrences such as this. Many times, places have a "devil" name for a reason, often dating back to Native American times.

***

JACOB GRAY – OLYMPIC NATIONAL PARK

. . .

TOWING a trailer full of camping gear, twenty-two-year-old Jacob Gray left Port Townsend alone on April 5, 2017, on his bicycle. Before heading east, he intended to visit Olympic National Park in Washington's Daniel J. Evans Wilderness.

On April 6, his bike, trailer, and most of his gear were found about six and a half miles up Sol Duc Hot Springs Road. Among the Quileute Indians, Sol Duc means sparkling water. Strangely, four arrows were sticking in the ground and one out of the back of the trailer, and a bow was on the ground as if it had just been nonchalantly tossed there. However, the owner of the bike and gear was nowhere to be found.

Ranger John Bowie checked the area around the bike that afternoon. Perhaps the cyclist went to the river for some water after making the short walk? The freezing water would have killed him if he slipped in and couldn't get out. Could the rider have hitchhiked his way up to the hot springs nearby? The scene was indeed puzzling to the ranger.

In the morning, Bowie called his colleague Brian Wray and asked him to recheck the area. Wray checked the site on April 8 and found the bike and trailer untouched.

Another year went by without any answers to the puzzling discovery. The mystery of Jacob's death remains unanswered. How did he end up 5,300 feet above sea level and at least fifteen miles away from where he left his bike near the top of a ridge above Hoh Lake?

Jacob Gray's bike and trailer were in excellent condition. Neither appeared to be damaged, and the trailer contained a lot of equipment. During their check of the Sol Duc Hot Springs Resort, the rangers found no trace of the owner; they felt certain he had fallen into the river, so they waited until the water was lower in the summer to examine the river.

Ranger Wray found Jacob Gray's telephone number list among the items on April 7 and called his sister, Mallory, to get more information. Mallory suggested that Wray call their parents in Santa Cruz immediately.

According to a family list, the trailer was missing a water filter and a Camelbak backpack that can hold plastic water containers.

Photographs were taken of the bike and trailer; then everything was loaded into a boathouse on Lake Crescent and inventoried.

Now the hunt for Jacob had begun. Several people and dogs from the Clallam County Sheriff's Office joined the search the next day, but no results were found.

Olympic Mountain Rescue volunteer trackers searched the area on Wednesday, April 12, 2017, nearly a week after the bike was found. A mossy rock showed evidence of someone switching from hiking boots to running shoes, walking to the river's edge, then slipping and falling in. A few hundred yards downstream, there were signs that someone had gotten out. The logjams in the river were searched by a state fisheries biologist rather than swift-water rescue divers.

As of 5 p.m. on Thursday, April 13, dog teams began searching. This was the time when it was evident that they were looking for a dead cyclist and not a live one. Cadaver dogs encountered a logjam that may have trapped a corpse beneath it. The log could also have been swabbed with scent molecules from cadaver matter washing in from the bank. However, all the logjams for twelve miles on either side of the bike area were searched, and Jacob's body was not found.

A limited continuous search was initiated on April 14 in Olympic National Park after searching continued throughout that week. By the time other jurisdictions got involved, the Olympic Ranger SAR operation was effectively over.

No helicopters from the Whidbey Island Naval Air Station, which helps with searches in Olympic National Park, were requested, nor were any aircraft with the Coast Guard based in Port Angeles. There are a huge amount of volunteer dog teams, and the family had lined up a ready team, but the park rejected it, believing that another volunteer team would be more suitable.

With the help of volunteers, Clallam County Search and Rescue began searching on Saturday, April 15. They covered the west bank of the river, a portion of Olympic National Forest, as well as in the park. In Port Angeles, to the east, and in Forks, to the west, flyers were posted on park information boards as well as in gas stations and convenience stores. On April 16, 2017, Clallam County began scaling back its search.

A pair of shorts in Jacob's size was found a few miles downstream, and he had been given a similar pair for Christmas, which was given to a Seattle crime lab for DNA analysis. Unfortunately, the results of the test were inconclusive.

The Sol Duc River was searched in July 2017 by more than one hundred search and rescue volunteers from Western Washington, but no clues were found.

More than a year later, on August 10, 2018, a team of biologists making a trip into the mountains to study marmots found Jacob's remains, including his clothes, wallet and additional gear in an area above Hoh Lake, which is a minimum of fifteen miles north of where his bike had been previously located.

It was likely avalanche-prone terrain in April, so his body wasn't found near a trail. It is likely that the bones were seen from the air, as they were found on a treeless ridge.

From the trailhead of Sol Duc, Hoh Lake is about ten miles away. Before reaching the lake, which is 5,300 feet above sea level, the trail passes through old-growth forests and alpine slopes.

Police found skeletal remains and more clothing in the area the next morning. According to Penny Wagner, spokesperson for Olympic National Park, the clothing matched what the family predicted Jacob would wear.

According to the Clallam County deputy coroner, the

King County Medical Examiner's Office confirmed the identity of the remains on August 18, 2018. Investigators initially did not suspect foul play when they found the remains in an area that was not described as a campsite.

Randy Gray, Jacob's father, said he wanted to believe his son was out working or fishing somewhere, still living his life, before the body was discovered. Jacob Gray was an avid outdoorsman who enjoyed camping alone. Randy had relentlessly searched for Jacob since his bike was found on Sol Duc Hot Springs Road. In addition to searching in the Sol Duc Valley, he said he searched in other parts of the country and in Canada as well.

It remains a mystery as to what happened to Jacob Gray.

Clallam County Deputy Coroner Christi Wojnowski determined an inconclusive official cause of death, as only dental records could identify the body. It was not possible for Gray to have an autopsy. At the scene where his body was discovered, he had a cigarette lighter, insulated clothing, and plenty of food. Since Jacob's remains showed no signs of trauma, the authorities believe he died of hypothermia.

There are many unanswered questions surrounding Jacob's disappearance. Here are a few to consider:

He planned and told people he was going east, so why did he turn around and go west without telling anyone?

What was the purpose of leaving the bike where it was, unlocked, in plain sight of traffic, with his gear out on the ground?

What was the reason for the four arrows sticking out of the ground?

Fifteen miles from where he left his bike in the snow and at least 5,300 feet above sea level, how did he manage to travel that distance?

What caused him to become hypothermic if he was properly clothed?

What was his intention at the time of his death in the wilderness—suicide perhaps?

Sadly, Jacob took all the answers with him.

STEFAN BISSERT – OLYMPIC NATIONAL PARK

ORIGINALLY FROM BAD OEYNHAUSEN, Germany, Stefan Bissert, twenty-three, studied at Oregon State University as a Fulbright scholar and exchange student. On January 20, 1992, he was hiking with another German exchange student in the Sol Duc area on the western side of the Olympic National Park. In their plans, they intended to hike four miles southwest of Sol Duc Hot Springs to Deer Lake.

Stefan and his hiking partner parted ways for some reason, so Bissert attempted to hike to the Hoh River trailhead twenty-three miles away. He was reported missing on January 21 by his friend when he didn't arrive.

Only wearing jeans, a shirt, and a windbreaker, he was

NATIONAL PARK MYSTERIES AND DISAPPEARANCES   109

not dressed or equipped to camp in the snow overnight. Only a few pieces of fruit were in the daypack, and he didn't have a hat, gloves, or camping equipment. Stefan would have run into a winter storm that hit the Olympic high country all week if he had indeed taken this route, as is believed.

Park rangers, dogs, and helicopters assisted with the search. Olympic Mountain Rescue members from Kitsap were among the volunteer searchers.

They searched for five days without success and called off the search after failing to find any clues about the missing hiker. A range of weather conditions were encountered by the search and rescue teams, including rain, sleet, hail, snow, cold, and extreme avalanche danger.

No trace of Stefan has ever been found.

BRYAN LEE JOHNSTON – OLYMPIC NATIONAL PARK

BRYAN LEE JOHNSTON, seventy-one, planned to hike the Ozette Loop Trail in Olympic National Park over two or three days. This park is on Washington State's Olympic Peninsula in the Pacific Northwest. The Ozette Trail consists of a nine-mile loop trail that leads three miles northwest to the Pacific Ocean, then three miles south along the beach, then another three miles inland.

In the early hours of August 22, 2013, Bryan got up early to go for a hike along the Ozette and left his sleeping wife a note. Bryan was never seen or heard from again.

Bryan was physically fit, and as a Cub Scout, Boy Scout, and Eagle Scout, he hiked regularly. Along with hiking, he loved taking photographs, going on cruise ships with his wife, and constructing things in his home workshop.

Since his white hair was so thick, it was easiest for him to pull it back into a ponytail, and he didn't wear glasses every day, although he was thought to have been wearing them at the time of his disappearance.

After earning a bachelor's degree from the University of Washington in 1966, he served in the Air Force until 1970 and then worked for Seattle City Light until his retirement.

The description of him as a quiet man, almost a loner, was given by family and close friends.

Blue eyes and a height of five feet ten inches characterized his appearance. He was wearing blue jeans and carrying a black daypack when last seen.

The rangers in Olympic National Park were notified that Bryan was missing by Bryan's wife and stepchildren on Wednesday, August 28, 2013.

On the plank trail, it is impossible to get lost. However, you may have some trouble negotiating a couple of steep headlands if the tides are high. But while on this loop, Bryan seems to have somehow become disoriented and then became lost.

Over fifty park rangers and teams from Clallam, Grays Harbor, and Pierce Counties searched the Ozette area for three days without finding Johnston.

Rangers found a truck parked at the Ozette trailhead with receipts from Port Angeles businesses dated August 22, 2013, the day he left his home in Ballard.

The ground search was called off with no clues. Family members said they think that Bryan didn't intend to disappear, but he was often described as someone who was very introspective and kept to himself most of the time. It's unsure as to what he was carrying in the black daypack he was using when he vanished.

His sister, Jinny Longfellow, said she believed Bryan may have checked out other hiking areas before trying out the Ozette Loop Trail, but then had an accident or became injured.

One of his boots was found on the trail in 2017 by a hiker and turned in to authorities, according to a family member. However, nothing else has turned up since, and Bryan's remains are yet to be found.

SHIRLEY BAUMANN – QUARTZ CREEK TRAIL

ON MONDAY, July 20, 2020, Shirley Baumann, sixty-one, hiked to Lake Blethen from Middle Fork Road in North Bend, Washington, using the Quartz Creek Trail.

Her return date was supposed to be Wednesday, July 22, but she didn't show back up.

Her habit of walking in the wilderness at least once a week led her to be an experienced hiker. With hazel eyes and blonde hair, she was five feet four inches tall and weighed about 145 pounds. She may have had brown sunglasses and/or reading glasses, and a cell phone (not a smartphone, but rather a flip-style model) on the day she disappeared.

A foot search is extremely difficult in this area due to its treacherous terrain and many steep cliffs.

Search and Rescue volunteers searched in the Snoqualmie River Middle Fork area of North Bend for over three thousand hours, according to King County Sheriff's Office Sergeant Ryan Abbott. Baumann's car was found at an area trailhead, and a friend stated that sniffer dogs picked up her scent near her campsite as well as on the trail.

Ground searches were suspended on July 28 while helicopter searches continued. No sign of Shirley was found, but her hiking equipment was located.

As this is a relatively new missing person case, no further information is available as of this writing in October of 2021. The case is ongoing, and it is strange that Shirley's gear has turned up, but no sign of her or any remains.

GIOVANNA "GIA" FUDA – SCENIC CREEK

ON SATURDAY, August 1, 2020, Giovanna "Gia" Fuda, eighteen, was found in good health. Nine days had gone by since the woman was last seen in the wilderness in Washington State.

According to the King County Sheriff's Office (KCSO), after leaving Maple Valley, Washington, the teenager left her home for a drive east of Skykomish, a town located about a seventy-mile drive east of Seattle. Somehow, she wandered beyond Seattle's views of the city and into a remote part of Washington.

Gia Fuda was last seen by her mother that morning. She did not return home or check in with her parents by 11:30 p.m., which worried her parents. She was not responding to their calls and texts. KCSO was notified at 1 in the morning, and a missing person report was filed.

As Gia walked into a coffee shop near the town of Index at 10 a.m. that early morning, she was captured on a surveillance camera. After purchasing a Bigfoot key chain, she left.

Three days after Gia disappeared, a Washington State Department of Transportation worker found her car nearby. Due to the car's odd placement, the worker noticed it right away. Gia Fuda's license plate number was checked, and the car turned out to belong to her. Gas had run out in the vehicle, authorities discovered. Her belongings and purse were still in the car.

Detectives with the KCSO Major Crimes Unit suspected foul play may have been involved in the disappearance. They feared she had possibly been abducted by a stranger. The car was parked where her cell phone had last pinged a tower.

Search and rescue teams from all over the state assisted with the search, which began on July 26, although pings were not able to track anyone in the area due to the cell phone dead zone. Participants included dog teams, mountain rescuers, and law enforcement officers from across the state. Signs were made, fliers were handed out at coffee shops, and they walked hiking trails looking for her. However, no trace of Gia or her belongings was found.

Search and rescue teams found some of Gia's possessions near Scenic Creek on August 1, as hope was beginning to fade that she would be found alive. These included shoes, a bible, a bag, and her cell phone. She was discovered alive and well moments later. According to KCSO officials, Gia was found sitting on a rock near the river, up a steep ravine.

The rescuers reported that she'd panicked when her 2008 silver Toyota Corolla ran out of gas and stopped near Scenic Falls and Stevens Pass. The young woman wandered into the Cascade Mountains with only the items she could carry with her: her cell phone, a bible, and a journal. Her purse and its contents were left behind. The sheriff's office said that a gas station in Skykomish was ten miles away, so she cut off some distance through the dense forest to get help. It was too risky to walk along the highway. Her journey took her through the forest, where she got lost.

Gia was treated at a local hospital for scratches, cuts, and dehydration, but was otherwise in good health.

Her survival was facilitated by warm nights and water from the creek, according to Greg Prothman, a rescue team leader, who also said she stayed roughly in the same area, which made finding her easier. Gia had also eaten a few berries, possibly huckleberries, but not too many for fear they were poisonous.

As wild and unforgiving as the wilderness in Washington State can be, Gia is quite fortunate indeed.

ANDREW DEVERS – NORTH BEND

IN THIS ENTRY, we'll delve into the story of a hiker and some of the strange experiences he encountered while spending an incredible nine days lost in the woods of the Cascades near North Bend, Washington.

June 18, 2020, started out just as any other day for Andrew Devers. It was a beautiful day, and Andrew had woken up that morning with hiking on his mind. So he hopped into his car and took off on what he believed would be a relaxing three-mile hike up the Pratt River Trail.

Andrew had solo hiked this short trail successfully more than a dozen times previously, so he thought nothing of taking off on a whim. He simply left his apartment without a phone, thinking his hike would be free from distracting technology. Without telling anyone where he was going or when he planned to return, he drove the short distance to North Bend's Middle Fork Trailhead. In retrospect, he now understands how foolhardy this folly was, and how it almost cost him his very life.

So he arrived and hit the trail with a water bottle, a thermos of coffee, two cans of Mountain Dew, and a couple of personal items. Andrew hadn't bothered to pack any food for the hike, instead looking forward to the can of SpaghettiOs that was waiting in his vehicle for after the hike was finished.

Speaking with a local news station, Andrew recalls, "I had a notebook with me and I was expecting to get to the top, read my book for a little bit, write a couple poems and then come back."

So Andrew hiked merrily along the trail, enjoying his time with nature...

But then, in what he says seemed like only a short time, Andrew was suddenly and inexplicably very lost.

Andrew said, "I was following what I thought was the trail and then I just remember being off in my own head for about forty minutes and then I look back and there's no trail..."

Andrew says that he believes he spent the first six hours or so alternating between trying to locate a familiar landmark and screaming for help, but to no avail.

After those first few hours, still very lost and no closer

to finding his way back onto the trail, it was growing dark. Andrew picked out a comfortable-looking spot beneath a tree so he could rest up and try to find his way come daylight. However, the next day was just as disorienting. Andrew became very frustrated that he wasn't having any luck finding his way out of the woods.

That day was essentially a repeat of the one before. By the time his third day rolled around, Andrew said his mind had begun to play tricks on him.

By June 22, it had already been four days since Andrew began his three-mile hike and seemingly disappeared. The King County Sheriff's Office (KCSO), had been made aware of Andrew's disappearance by this point, and along with trained search and rescue volunteers, they began to search the area. The Middle Fork Trailhead was closed to prevent any interference with the SAR efforts, and a tweet was released requesting information from the public.

As the days continued to pass, Andrew was still unable to find his way out, or even find anything that looked halfway familiar.

Andrew stated at times, he remembers hearing a person's voice calling out to him from across the river. He couldn't see the person, but when he tried to cross, he ended up falling in and was carried downstream. Eventually he was able to grab hold of a low-hanging tree limb and pull himself from the water. It was in this area that he discovered the first food he'd seen in days.

Andrew says, "I swear I heard my girlfriend's voice and

I look to the right and there's this like perfect red berry and then I follow these berries and it leads to this personal oasis that I was able to recover in, because at this point my legs and everything were all messed up but I didn't have food until then."

Andrew continued explaining the "miracle berries": "They tasted phenomenal, they tasted like life, like I could feel the life going back into my body."

The berries helped settle the hunger gnawing at his belly, but after what seemed like days of prowling the woods for more and drinking water from the river to satisfy his thirst, Andrew could feel hope once again slipping away.

"I was like screaming and no one was listening to me, no one was replying."

Several times, Andrew spotted helicopters flying just above the treetops, but was unable to catch their attention.

"I feel like a ghost, like I can hear everything, but no one can hear me, and there's choppers but they can't see me," Andrew wrote in his notebook.

The days continued to pass, and he continued his written account of being lost in the woods. At the beginning of his ordeal, Andrew even wrote ideas for YouTube videos and other creative ideas that popped into his head. When he first spotted the helicopter, he penned a poem for the pilot he could see inside, begging him for help. As the days of solitude wore on and hope seemed to fade, he even wrote out his wedding vows so that if he didn't make it out, his girlfriend of seven years would hopefully find solace in knowing that he had, indeed, intended to marry her.

"Day seven and day eight, I was like, 'okay, I'm actually dying, be fair to the people you're leaving behind,'" Andrew said.

"I was accepting I was dying," he continued. "I think the saddest part is no one was going to be there."

It was on the ninth day that Andrew made a last grasp at survival.

He spotted a small stream and planned to follow it as far as he could, hopefully spotting a trail or another hiker. Otherwise, he knew he'd just have to lie down beside it and accept his fate.

Surprisingly, the stream idea worked. Andrew said, "I ended up randomly just like crawling over a tree and finding like an acorned path."

Although he wasn't aware of it at the time, the "acorned path," as he described it, was actually the very same trail he'd gotten lost from nine days prior.

Overjoyed and emotional at finding a trail at long last, Andrew said he collapsed alongside it, too tired to move any further. "I just slept and I woke up and these two like jacked hiker bros were like, 'what's going on, man?' and it was like everything I wanted, it was like waking up to my own *Baywatch* scene," Andrew said.

Oddly enough, Andrew was found only about two miles from the trailhead where he'd started when the hikers discovered him. They recognized Andrew was in serious trouble, and one of them raced back to his car and sped until he was within cell phone reception, where he placed a call for help.

"It was hard to believe someone was actually there until the rescue workers were calling my name and then I was like, 'Is that my name? That's my name! It's me, it's Andrew!'"

Andrew says that now it's all a blur and he can't remember what the SAR volunteers even said to him, but he does remember feeling a sense of relief wash over him knowing that, as he strangely worded it, "a human finally had control over the situation."

Crews took Andrew out of the woods to the trailhead. From there, he was then rushed to an area hospital, where he was evaluated and later released.

Two days after his rescue, Andrew gave an interview to a local news crew. Although he stated that he was feeling well, he was still dealing with severe dehydration, some muscle atrophy, and said that he often had periods of feeling weak.

"Physically, apparently I'm fine," Andrew told the reporter. "It's just the emotional thing that's the bigger thing now.

"I remember the man with the piercing green eyes and the woman with the accent and the man who was behind me that was carrying me with the drill sergeant voice and then the other dude with like the perfect red-headed beard and then the woman who's 99-percent a nurse but not fully registered yet... I'm just never going to forget you

NATIONAL PARK MYSTERIES AND DISAPPEARANCES   121

guys, and I have a brain that naturally forgets, so I hope that means a lot... I'm just glad I'm here," he said.

Andrew further went on to tell the reporter that he still sometimes feels this is all a dream.

"It just feels like I'm not fully awake," Andrew said, standing outside his apartment in Tukwila.

"I don't believe myself, like even now there's a person with a camera and you, like five days ago I'm accepting that I'm dead," he said, shaking his head from side to side. Just two days ago, he had been lost in the Cascade Mountains and facing death, but now here he was again, with a second chance at life.

"I stopped thinking about weeks and months and years and it only came down to hours," Andrew said. "It was like nine days of me versus me," "There were so many moments when I was like, 'this is it, you're out!' you know... and then it's like your hopes are shattered."

When fully recovered, Andrew states he has a desire to become a search and rescue volunteer, so he can pay it forward and come full circle from his ordeal.

FOUR

MISSING IN OLYMPIC NATIONAL PARK AND FOREST

Olympic National Forest and Park was established on June 29, 1938, residing in the Upper Peninsula of Washington state. The ecosystem hosts several protected species of flora and fauna, including the Western Hemlock and the Snowshoe Hare. Designated in 1976 as an International Biosphere Reserve and in 1971 as a World Heritage Site, almost three million people visit the Reserve every year. There are over six hundred miles of hiking trails within the park from which visitors can see waterfalls, old-growth forests, and the Pacific Ocean, where people can do whale watching, and it is also home to one of the last temperate Rain Forests in the United States. Olympic National Park has one of the most diverse ecosystems in the United States, there are over sixty active glaciers and over six hundred archaeological sites within the park boundaries. Having over one million acres to explore, it's certainly not the largest or most visited of the National Parks but is one of the most desired for day hikes due to the easy accessibility of trails. The easy accessibility and diverse landscapes could be why some of the most baffling missing persons cases in the National Parks chain come from Olympic National Forest/Park and Recreation area. Here are just a few of the cases that remain unsolved to this day.

DUANE MILES- ON TUESDAY, October 19, 2021, seventy-eight-year-old Duane Miles of Beaver, Washington, was on a day hike around Olympic National Park/ Amanda Park area headed to Graves Creek Corral looking for elk sheds with friends before going missing. Four days later, Miles was reported missing by family on October 23, 2021, after failing to meet with friends later in the day on the 19th as planned. Search and Rescue crews were on the ground searching for the experienced hiker on October 23rd, almost immediately after the report was filed. Duane Miles was very familiar with the Graves Creek area as he hiked those trails, often leaving designated paths to seek out shed antlers in other areas of the park. Teams searched for the lost hiker throughout the week and through the weekend with dog teams and Coast Guard helicopters, but there was no sign of the missing man. The weather turned inclement over the weekend with rain and snow mix, hampering search efforts. Mile's truck was found in the Graves Creek Campground parking lot with no evidence of any activity around it. The following week, the search was scaled back due to weather and search crews finding no trace in the extensive week-long search. On November 1, 2021, searchers found a freshly opened can of sardines in the initial search area. It is unknown if the can belonged to Duane Miles or if another hiker in the area left it behind. Duane Miles was declared dead in December of 2021, on the date he went missing. His family held a memorial in his honor, speaking of his service to the United States in the Army, his dedication to helping kids in an outdoor program, and was an expert hiker, survival expert, and hunter. He is terribly missed by those that knew and loved him. Duane Ellis Miles was seventy-eight years old and was last seen wearing black rain pants, a camouflage jacket, and a dark-colored backpack. He was described as 5.9, 185 lbs., and had blue eyes. Authorities are asking anyone that was in the Graves Creek area on October 19, 2019, and saw Miles to contact the National Park Service at (888)-653-0009 as this is still an active missing person's case, search, and recovery.

GILBERT "GIL" **Mark Gilman-** On Saturday, June 24, 2006, forty-seven-year-old Gilman Mark Gilman, also known as "Gil", went on a short walk in Olympic National Park and was never seen again. Gilman had quite a colorful history as he was an Army ex-paratrooper, having served his duties in Panama, East Africa, and Israel. In his military career, he was also a part of the 82nd Airborne Squad and was awarded two bronze stars. "Gil," as his family and friends referred to him, studied at the Solvay Business School in Brussels, the London School of Economics, and at Union College in New York, although it is unknown what his specialty was or if he received a degree. Gilman was fluent in several different languages, Arabic, Russian, and Chinese, which aided him in his time as a military interrogator and counterterrorism/intelligence. While in Iraq, he was also a contractor for a year. After his time in the Middle East, Gilman returned to New York, where he worked for the United Nations, then went on to Washington to work for Sandy Matheson on the 2004 Congressional Campaign, who was the director of the Department of Retirement Systems. Then in 2005, he worked with Matheson as Deputy Director of Retirement Systems, counseling her on pension issues nationally as well as locally. Suffice to say that Gilbert Gilman was a vital person to the Government of the United States. When Gilman went missing, he was taking some much needed and desired time off from his stressful occupation to relax and unwind. That led him to the Staircase Rapids Loops Trail in Olympic National Park on that faithful day. When Gilman arrived at his destination, he was greeted by Park Ranger Sanny Lustig. "I could actually hear the music playing in his car and went out to see what was going on, and I had a brief conversation with him and asked him to turn down the music. I got the sense he was going for a hike," Lustig said in an interview with authorities. The Staircase Loops Trail is just over a two-mile hike and is an old-growth forest area of Olympic National Park, which hindered ariel searches because of the large Western Hemlock, Western Red Cedar, and Douglas Firs, some of which are over three to four hundred-years-old. These massive trees provide a "canopy" type blanket over the area that even ground search and rescue teams have a hard time navigating. Sitting just thirty minutes outside the town of Hoodsport, Washington, "The Trails" is also a seasonal Rangers Station and a campground. Aside from the Staircase Loops Trail, there is also the North Fork Skokomish River Trail which can be accessed via Staircase Loops Trail, where there is a swinging bridge across the Skokomish River and visitors can enjoy another fifteen miles of hiking. The day after his planned hike, Gilman was supposed to accompany Sandy Matheson to a meeting in Spokane, Washington. When he failed to show up, he was reported missing. A 2005 Ford Thunderbird convertible confirmed as belonging to Gilbert Gilman was found at the Staircase Rangers Station. Search and Rescue crews, along with a helicopter, and a search plane equipped with FLIR scent dogs, all joined a sixty-two-man crew to search for Gilman through thick forest, trails, steep, rocky terrain, and the Skokomish River for eleven days. On day ten, the official search was called off, and Gilbert Gilman was declared lost by the United States Forestry Service and authorities. No clues ever surfaced as to his whereabouts, and all his bank cards and accounts have remained untouched. Several theories were discussed, from Gilman leaving on his own accord to a possible kidnapping because of his military background. Other theories included

Gilman having been murdered by a serial killer, animal predation, an accident on the trail, or a medical mishap. None of these theories have ever been confirmed. On August 27, 2015, forty-seven-year-old Gilbert Mark Gilman was declared deceased after his mother, Doris Gilman, petitioned the Thurston County Superior Court for his death certificate and to become the trustee of his estate. The court granted Mrs. Gilman's request as the case met the criteria for a missing person to be declared deceased by the state of Washington, which is seven years of no clues or contact from the person and no satisfactory explanation as to what happened to them when they went missing. Despite authorities' best efforts in search and rescue and search and recovery, nothing was ever found. It's as if Gilman walked into the park and into the unknown. The Israel Keyes Theory- the serial killer was one major theory that investigators entertained because the known serial killer, Israel Keyes, lived in Washington at the time Gilman disappeared and was known to hike in the same area. Keyes was arrested in Texas after being pulled over in a rented car. He was accused of murdering a woman in Alaska. Through questioning by a Texas State Trooper that was aware that Keyes could be in the area after police from Alaska were tracking him via his debit card purchases in the Lower 48. Keyes confessed to killing eighteen-year-old Samantha Koenig after abducting her from a coffee kiosk in Anchorage, Alaska, in 2012, leaving shortly after on vacation with his girlfriend and daughter. Keyes also confessed to killing a couple in Vermont. There would never come a chance to question Keyes about his possible involvement in the Gilman case. In 2012, Israel Keyes was found non-responsive by jail guards in his holding cell. He left a picture painted in a red body fluid that depicted eleven skulls that stated, "We are now one." M, William Phelps, Author and Host of Dark Minds, investigated this angle of the Gilman case and concluded that Keyes was a good suspect in his case as Keyes had been issued several backcountries permits for Olympic National Park and was living in Neah Bay, Washington at the time Gilman went missing. However, in March 1994, this theory was disputed by Federal Bureau of Investigations Special Agent Kevin Donovan, citing conflicting evidence given by Keyes and other witnesses. Gilbert Mark Gilman was just forty-seven years old when he went missing. He is described as 5.7, 155-165 lbs., with grey/brown hair and brown eyes. If you or anyone you ay know has any clues as to the whereabouts of Gilman or saw him on Saturday, June 24, 2006, you are asked to contact the United States National Park Service Olympic National Park at (360)-565=3130 and reference Gilbert Gilman.

JOHN DEVINE-ON FRIDAY, September 6, 1997, seventy-three-year-old John Devine from Sequim, Washington, set out to climb Mount Baldy in Olympic National Park via the Maynard Burn Trail, a notoriously steep and rugged area. Devine was last seen on the Grey Wolf Ridge in the North part of the park. After not making it to his next meeting point on September 7, Devine's family reported him missing. A search was promptly launched, and nine search and rescue volunteers boarded a helicopter to do an aerial sweep, but crashed shortly after take-off, killing four members and injuring five others. Inclement weather was cited for the crash, which at the time was snow and wind. With the change in weather and the accident, volunteers were limited to ground searches. They continued searching through the weather in the Muller Creek area on September 12, 1997, but were brought off the mountain before nightfall. The search for John Devine was officially called off on September 13, 1997. Clallam County Sheriff's Deputy Sgt. Don Kelly stated, "If he were walking around up there, we would have found him by now. And if he had fallen and hurt himself, he probably wouldn't be alive." In the same interview, Park Service volunteer Jason Berry also said, "It's steep and rugged...the bushes are super thick and, it's tough to walk down the drainages." John Devine was seventy-two years old and is described as an expert hiker. Details of Devine's disappearance were limited to just a few paragraphs, but it was noted that he was legally blind in one eye, but this "never slowed him down," his wife stated. The investigation into the crash of the search and rescue helicopter was ongoing at the time of this article but was eventually thought to be a weight issue that caused it to go down.

JACOB GRAY- ON APRIL 5, 2017, thirty-year-old Jacob Gray, originally from Santa Cruz, California but at the time resided in Port Townsend, Washington, left his home on his bike with a trailer attached. His plan was to camp and hike in the Daniel J. Evans Wilderness Area of Olympic National Park. On the same day, a Forest Ranger, John Bowie, found Gray's equipment about six and a half miles up Sol Duc Hot Springs Road. Upon inspection, the Ranger found a bow on the ground and arrows sticking out of the back of the trailer and into the ground. Bowie called for backup as the scene looked unsettling. The bike, trailer, and contents were in working and perfect order, and he could tell the items hadn't been there long. When Ranger Brian Wray arrived to check the area the next morning on June 7, 2017, nothing had been touched. The bike and all its contents had not been moved. The Rangers checked the nearby trail to the river and noticed fresh foot tracks and what looked like a place where the moss had been disturbed on a rock, a possible slip-and-fall scenario. The Rangers also checked the local Hot Springs where visitors like to relax, thinking maybe Gray had hitched a ride there. Upon questioning patrons, no one remembered seeing anyone that hadn't been there the last few days. The Rangers returned to the bike and trailer, seizing them for safe storage until the mystery could be solved. Among the contents found was a list of phone numbers that the Rangers used to reach out to Gray's family members. They were able to contact his sister and were instructed then to contact Gray's parents in Santa Cruz, California. Officer Wray learned that Jacob Gray had plans to camp in the area where his belongings were found but that family members hadn't heard from him since he had contacted them about the trip. The parents were asked to make a list of their son's belongings so that Rangers could determine if anything was missing. The only items that weren't found were a Camelback water container and a water filtration system. This led Rangers to believe that the" slip and fall" scenario they initially believed was even more of a possibility. It appears Gray walked to the river to fill his Camelback, where he slipped and fell into the swollen, icy river, which was experiencing Spring run-off levels. If the water were to be searched, officials would have to wait until the water receded later in the Summer. The Clallam County Sheriff's Office took over the investigation on June 7, 2017. A search party consisting of thirty people converged on the site where Gray went missing with search dogs, ready to comb the area for any clues that may lead to his whereabouts. Nothing was found in the initial search, so the Clallam County Sheriff's Office requested the help of trackers from Olympic Mountain Rescue. On Wednesday, April 12, 2017, a full week after Gray's bike was discovered, volunteer trackers found evidence of someone changing out of tennis shoes into boots, "walked to the river's edge, slipped and fell, leaving a mark on a mossy rock." Search and Rescue spread out, and another thirty yards downstream, they found evidence of someone getting out of the water. Search and Rescue completed their search later that week, not having found anything else to aid in the search. To the disappointment of all involved, the search mindset was changed from a rescue mission to recovery. On Thursday, April 13, 2017, teams began searching log jams in the river for a body. Dogs hit on a particular set of logs, but there was nothing found. After that, the Search and Recover teams were placed on a limited continuous search. Surprisingly, air support was never requested, and the Gray family had another volunteer party ready to go, but the Park Service declined the help, stating, "they had another volunteer group in mind," but it was reported that they were even "hesitant to request" help from their choice of teams. On Saturday, April 15, 2017, Clallam County Search and Rescue initiated another search on the East side of the river, along Olympic National Forest as well as the Park. Fliers were placed at Park kiosks, in the town of Forks, on telephone poles and in stores with information about Jacob Gray. However, the Clallam County Search was scaled down by the next day. During the remaining search on the 16th, "a pair of Burnside brand shorts were found a couple of miles downstream" that were like a pair that Gray had received for Christmas the prior year. They were sent off for DNA testing. In July 2017, the last official search was conducted as a final push to find the remains of Jacob Gray. However, volunteers never found any more clues, and the search was called off. Over a year passed before the case would have any movement on it. On August 10, 2018, biologists that were conducting a study on mountain marmots came upon human remains and contacted authorities. The discovery was positively identified as Jacob Gray. His wallet, gear, and clothing were all found at the site. This provided closure to the family but brought about a whole new set of questions because the items, along with Gray, were found on a ridge overlooking Hoh Lake and fifteen miles away from where his bike and trailer were found and were nowhere near a trail. Authorities descended on the area the next day and found skeletal remains, clothing the family identified, and the gear that the biologists reported. The family was grief-stricken as they had held out hope that Jacob would be found alive and living out in the wilderness somewhere. His father, Randy Gray, stated he had searched the Sol Duc Valley all over the country and even Canada. The Medical Examiner did a full autopsy but was unable to determine the manner or means of how Gray died. They speculated that it was from hypothermia, but he was found with adequate clothing for the weather and time of year. Many questions remain about the disappearance of Jacob Gray. He told his family he was traveling East and was found far West; why? He left most of his equipment in the Sol Duc Road area and only took a few items, which contained food, clothing, and water. This case remains a mystery to this day, and many that worked on the case stated that "these questions may never be answered."

BRYAN LEE JOHNSTON- ON AUGUST 22, 2013, seventy-one-year-old Bryan Lee Johnston set out to the Ozette Loop Trail in Olympic National Park for a two-to-three-day camping/hiking trip. That morning, the avid and fit hiker woke up, gathered his equipment, left his wife a note, and drove away, never to be seen again. A young Bryan Johnston worked his way through the Scouts, becoming an Eagle Scout, which he was proud of. The promising young man attended the University of Washington, earning his bachelor's in engineering. He also served in the Air Force from 1966 until 1970, finally settling at Seattle City Light as an Engineer until he retired. On August 28, 2013, Johnston's wife reported him missing to the Rangers at Olympic National Park. The trail he was supposed to take was a "plank trail," a path through the park that is wooden and "almost impossible to get lost on," stated Park Rangers. Fifty Park Rangers and volunteers from three counties spent three days searching the Ozette Loop Trail area for the missing grandfather, only finding his truck parked at the Ozette Trailhead. Jinny Longfellow, Johnston's oldest sister, suggested that he may have visited other trails before going to Ozette, but there are so many within the park it would be impossible to search them all. In 2017, a boot likened to that of which Johnston was reported as wearing was found by a hiker, but no other clues have been found since then. As of the release of this script, there have been no other clues as to where Bryan Johnston may be. He is described as a fit seventy-one-year-old with white hair, blue eyes, 5.10, last seen carrying a black pack and wearing blue jeans. If you or someone you know has any information on or saw Bryan Johnston on August 22, 2013, you are asked to contact the United States National Park Service Olympic National Park at (360)-565=3130 and reference Bryan Lee Johnston.

WORKS CITED:

- Missing Olympic National Park hiker: Duane Miles search update | king5.com
- The puzzling disappearance of ex-paratrooper Gilbert Gilman from Olympic National Park — StrangeOutdoors.com
- The strange disappearance of John Devine from Olympic National Park — StrangeOutdoors.com
- The strange death of the cyclist Jacob Gray in the Olympic National Park — StrangeOutdoors.com
- The bizarre disappearance of Bryan Lee Johnston from the Olympic National Park — StrangeOutdoors.com

FIVE

HAUNTED WASHINGTON

Monte Cristo Ghost Town
Granite Falls, WA 98252
https://www.wta.org/go-hiking/hikes/monte-cristo-143

Looking for an abandoned ghost town to explore on a ghost hike? The old mining town of Monte Cristo can be found in the Cascade Mountains near Seattle. The harsh wilderness of the Cascades never gave this small town a fighting chance. The streets to the town were blocked during the summer months after frequent fires and floods destroyed outbuildings. The town eventually fell into disrepair, and the road has become impassable. However, you can still hike into the town and explore what is left of the ruins. The ghosts of long-gone miners are said to haunt the town.

The Whitman Massacre National Historic Site
328 Whitman Mission Road
Walla Walla, WA 99362
https://www.nps.gov/whmi/index.htm

KNOWN FOR ITS WINERIES, world-class food, and beautiful downtown, Walla Walla may not have always been this peaceful. However, in 1847, a massive massacre triggered the Cayuse War, which lasted for seven years and was marked by numerous battles between both sides.

Whitman was visited by several men disguised as doctors on November 29, 1847, armed with hatchets and guns. The Whitmans and a dozen others were killed by sixty Cayuse and Umatilla Indians in the ensuing attack at the mission. Fifty-three people were taken hostage as well.

It is said that the site is haunted, and hooves are still heard at various spots throughout the property. If you are interested in learning about the history of the area or experiencing paranormal activity, this is the place to go.

Greenwood Cemetery
113-633 Government Way, Spokane, WA 99224
https://spokanehistorical.org/items/show/77

SPOKANE HAS MANY TOURIST ATTRACTIONS, but one of the most haunted is Greenwood Cemetery. As a result of a legend that no one has managed to climb the staircase, it is known as "One Thousand Steps." It's said that the staircase is so haunted that even the bravest of souls will turn around in fear when they try to ascend it. The ghostly apparitions of many men, women, and children have been observed. Visitors have also heard shrieking and felt a strange wetness on their skin. More than a few stories surround the haunting's cause.

The Brick Saloon
100 W Pennsylvania Ave, Roslyn, WA 98941
(509) 649-2643

KITTITAS COUNTY, Washington, is home to the historic town of Roslyn. Constructed in 1889, the Brick Saloon serves up great food, has been featured in the television series *Northern Exposure* and the film *Runner Stumbles*, and is also famous for its hauntings. A little girl and a cowboy have appeared to both Brick employees and customers alike, and the piano in the back room is often heard playing when no one is there.

The Campbell House
Northwest Museum of Arts and Culture
2316 W 1st Ave, Spokane, WA 99201
(509) 456-3931

CAMPBELL HOUSE WAS ONCE the home of wealthy mining investors, but now it has been transformed into a museum of mid-twentieth-century domestic life. The history of the house, however, also contains some macabre elements. Three of Campbell's children were murdered by a burglar in the early 1900s, and a fourth was kidnapped. Residents have reported feeling irrational dread as well as cold spots. Perhaps it is one of the children's ghosts walking through the halls?

Old Cascade Tunnel
Leavenworth, WA 98826

ONE OF THE largest railroad disasters in US history occurred in the old Cascade Tunnel. The ruins of the abandoned tunnel can be found along the scenic Iron Goat Trail. The tunnel collapsed in 1910 after an avalanche swept two trains off their tracks. Ninety-six people were killed. However, people have reported hearing disembodied voices from outside the tunnel and along the trail, even though the old tunnel is not safe to enter.

As one of the creepiest locations in America, the Old Cascade Tunnel is located east of Everett in King County. There are stories of ghosts haunting it from the 1910 Wellington disaster.

For the purpose of removing eight switchbacks, the tunnel was completed in 1900. There were 2.6 miles of tracks, and the grade was 1.7% (1 in 58.8 ft). This tunnel is dangerous because it is caving in. No matter what you might hear or see, DO NOT ENTER the tunnel under ANY circumstances! Sadly, the east end of the tunnel collapsed in 2006, causing most of the tunnel's demise. A stagnant lake formed around that end.

The tunnel lining collapsed about six hundred feet in from the west portal in the winter of 2006/2007. The tunnel has been completely blocked by a rock and debris dam, resulting in a small lake backing up behind the dam. In the vicinity of the failure, there is a crack and a split in the tunnel lining, which may result in it failing again at any time. Repeat, entry is prohibited into the tunnel for any reason. At the west end, a viewpoint has been constructed in an area that should be safe if a second collapse occurs.

The Yesler Building
400 Yesler Way
Seattle, WA 98104
https://kingcounty.gov/about/contact-us/locations/
Yesler.aspx

KNOWN as one of Washington's most haunted buildings, the Yesler building is notorious for its ghostly presence. Henry Yesler, a Seattle pioneer and the namesake of Yesler Way, wasn't just a millionaire and an early mayor of the city—he was also a spiritualist who believed that the living were capable of communicating with the dead.

During these seances, Yesler and his wife, Sarah, were allegedly channeling their late son George with help from astrologer friend William Henry Chaney. According to legend, the building was designed to allow spirits and other non-earthly beings to reside there.

The building once housed the city's jail as well as an emergency hospital in 1909. It was located on the lowest level of the building, just underneath the bridge, with an entrance off of Fourth Avenue.

PART 3

IDAHO

SIX

MYSTERIOUS DISAPPEARANCES

FERN LOVETT BAIRD – SAWTOOTH NATIONAL FOREST

IN THE AFTERNOON OF MONDAY, October 19, 2020, at around 1 p.m., Fern Lovett Baird, sixty-two, of Park City, Utah, signed in at the Prairie Creek Trailhead north of Ketchum, Idaho, and then she vanished. Fern's disappearance was reported to the authorities on October 22.

Fern was signed into the trail register at the same time as another hiker group. Was anyone else involved? The authorities have failed to locate them. Perhaps Fern took a trail that was quite different from Prairie Loop's relatively straightforward trail, but why? Despite an exhaustive search of the area, no trace of Fern has been found over a year after she disappeared.

The concierge at the hotel where Fern Baird stayed last saw her wearing a gray jacket, black pants, and carrying a black fanny pack, and she was captured on the surveillance system as she left the hotel.

Although experienced with hiking, she had no experience with mountaineering or technical hikes. It is likely that she would have stayed on the marked trails since she was not a risk-taker but a casual hiker who did not go bushwhacking or take shortcuts.

In the Salt Lake Valley and at Utah's mountain resorts, Fern owned Powder Beach Realty, specializing in residential sales and vacation rentals. In addition, she founded Yopa Bags to design and manufacture yoga-related backpacks.

After driving fifteen and a half miles north of Ketchum on Highway 75, you'll find the Prairie Creek Trailhead on Baker Creek Road #162 in the mountains.

From the Prairie Creek Trailhead, you can access the Prairie Lakes and Miner Lakes trails. In total, the Prairie Lakes trail measures five miles, or eight kilometers, each way. Through meadows and forests mixed with pine trees, the Prairie Lakes trail circles a creek. To reach the grassy basin where the lakes lie, there is a steady climb, but it is not difficult.

Sawtooth National Forest covers 2,110,408 acres in Idaho and partially in Utah, where this trail is located. On May 29, 1905, President Theodore Roosevelt established the Sawtooth Forest Reserve. Approximately nine hundred square miles of the forest, including the wilderness areas of Sawtooth, Cecil D. Andrus, White Clouds, and Hemingway-Boulders, were designated as Sawtooth National Recreation Area (SNRA) on August 22, 1972.

In addition to the Sawtooth Mountains, which traverse a part of the forest, the Sawtooth National Forest has the Albion Mountains, Black Pine Mountains, Boulder Mountains, Pioneer Mountains, Raft River Mountains, Smoky Mountains, Soldier Mountains, and White Cloud Mountains.

The Smoky Mountains are located in central Idaho, and Prairie Creek Peak is just one of only a few peaks in the Smoky Mountains that are over ten thousand feet high. Its most attractive feature is its north face, which rises one thousand feet steeply, above Prairie Lakes, forming a perfect pyramid shape. While its east slopes are less impressive, it forms Big Lost Lake's backdrop, while its jagged south ridge provides a bold contrast to Smoky Lake's area.

In spite of Prairie Creek Peak's proximity to the rest of the Smoky Mountains, few people make their way to its summit, either because of its rugged appearance or because of the difficult access to the peak.

Fern would have had the opportunity to take the wrong trail easily if she had been confused while hiking, something hikers in the area report often. Disorientation could have easily happened to her if she had lost her way or became too cold.

Around the same time that Fern signed the trail logbook, a group of hikers from Tulsa signed it as well. On

October 19, the group may have hiked either West Fork Prairie Creek drainage or Prairie Lake.

According to Blaine County Sheriff's Lieutenant Mike Abaid, "Fern Baird had checked in and after that, there was a party of five and it's not that legible, but what we are kind of making out is the last name is Adkins."

After being notified that Fern was missing, Blaine County Sheriff Search and Rescue members (BCSAR) and BCSO deputies began searching for her Thursday afternoon, October 22, 2020. When she failed to return to check out after asking the front desk about good hiking locations, the hotel notified the sheriff's office that day.

Her Subaru Crosstrek 2018 was discovered in Prairie Creek's parking lot. In the Prairie Peak area, north of Ketchum, Idaho, Fern had a number of hiking options from the trailhead.

Several National Guard helicopters, two drones, three K-9 units, as well as numerous searchers on foot, motorcycles, and horses were used to help find Fern. Lieutenant Mike Abaid said, "People have gotten turned around and lost out there before. I mean it's big country Idaho mountains."

At elevations ranging from 7,100 feet to 9,200 feet, searchers focused on Prairie Lakes, Minor Lakes, Norton Lakes, and Mill Lake. A fresh blanket of mountain snow covered the ground, and early winter conditions challenged the high-elevation search.

There was one last major search made on October 30, 2020, when Blaine County Sheriff Search and Rescue

(BCSAR) airlifted seven K-9 teams into the search area from 7,100 to 9,200 feet, along with ground search crews, and the search was officially called off.

Sheriff Steve Harkins of Blaine County stated, "This is not the outcome that we were hoping for, but after ten days of searching, we have exhausted our resources. We will continue to investigate any leads we gather."

In the days and weeks that have passed since she went missing, neither her credit cards nor her cell phone have been used, nor has there been any activity online.

SUSAN SEYMOUR ADAMS – SELWAY-BITTERROOT WILDERNESS

SUSAN ADAMS, forty-two, disappeared on September 30, 1990, after camping with her husband, Tom, near Battle Lake in the Selway-Bitterroot Wilderness in eastern Idaho. In a nearby meadow, she went bird-watching, and even though tracks were found, she was never seen again.

In addition to spending time outdoors, Tom and Susan like to go on trips together. After researching and planning for months, they had paid and arranged for a tour company, Iron Horse Outfitters, to help them explore the wilderness near the Idaho-Montana border. Although Susan wasn't an experienced outdoors person, according to her husband, she was excited about the trip and enjoyed being in the woods.

On Saturday, September 22, 1990, they arrived in Idaho Falls and headed to Hamilton, Montana, where Art Griffith, owner of the outfitting business, was waiting for them. On Wednesday, the group rode by horseback into Battle Lake, near the Bitterroot Divide, where they spent seven hours at the outfitter's camp.

During the group's stay at camp, they enjoyed some bird-watching, hunting, and other activities. Tom's hunting guide and he set out on an overnight trip on September 29, one week after his arrival in Idaho. In contrast to Tom, Susan remained at base camp since she was not as adventurous. Their hunt began at a ridge above the campsite, where Susan accompanied them with another guide. With the horses, Susan returned to camp with the guide. Tom did not see Susan again after that.

In the northwest corner of the United States, in Idaho and Montana, is the Selway-Bitterroot Wilderness. It is one of the largest wilderness areas in the United States, covering 1.3 million acres. The Bitterroot Mountain Range spans Idaho and Montana, and parts of the Bitterroot National Forest, Clearwater National Forest, Lolo National Forest, and Nez Perce National Forest are included. There are rocky alpine parks and coniferous forests in the high elevations surrounding the Bitterroot peaks.

Susan told the chef at base camp on Sunday, September 30 that she was going to go bird-watching in a

NATIONAL PARK MYSTERIES AND DISAPPEARANCES   151

nearby meadow. Except for the camouflage-print clothing she was wearing and her camera and binoculars, she left with no gear.

Susan's husband, Tom, returned from his hunting trip later that afternoon and learned Susan had gone bird-watching. After she didn't return, he became concerned when the evening approached, and hiked into the meadow to search for her.

Her footprints led him down a dusty trail as he hiked in the direction of the meadow. Before reaching the meadow, her footprints abruptly ended, as if she had suddenly disappeared. In a police report a month later, he wrote, "I followed the footprints to a place about 20 yards from the meadow, where the tracks stopped."

Despite searching all night for Susan, Tom and the tour guides did not find her. One of the guides rode on horseback to town to alert the authorities the next morning.

Searches on the ground and in the air were unsuccessful. Tuesday morning, snow and a cold wind hindered the search. The search was suspended until the weather improved. After continuing for three days, the search ended for the winter due to inclement weather.

Susan's remains were searched for once again in July 1991, using dogs and trackers. Captain Skott Mealer of the Idaho County Sheriff's Department said that it was the largest search he had ever seen in Idaho County. "There was a lot of pressure," he said.

The governor of Texas, whom Susan's husband worked

for, got involved, requesting helicopters from the National Guard to aid in the search for Susan.

The search meant a lot to the governor, who went on a fast for the duration of the search. Mealer said, "He figured if Susan was out there hungry, he would be too."

The searchers literally walked at arm's length from each other across acres of wilderness during the second search. A track was found leading to the conclusion that the person had been injured.

"There is now a difference in the track and prints," the search report states. "The left foot is turned out, like an injury. Possible fracture or sprain of the left lower extremity."

A psychic described the area to be searched. "I feel as if she is within a three-to-five-mile distance and in the direction of north to northwest of her campsite," the psychic claimed. According to her, Susan died from head injuries sustained from falling off a rock cliff.

"I believe beyond any reasonable doubt that Susan Adams died from injuries or other related causes due to being lost or hurt in the wilderness area near Battle Lake," Sheriff Randy Baldwin wrote in his final report on the investigation. "I also believe that Susan Adams' remains are still in that area, but feel that any future organized search would not be effective in locating her remains."

Tom, Susan's husband, was originally considered a suspect, but he and the rest of the party members passed polygraphs.

NATIONAL PARK MYSTERIES AND DISAPPEARANCES   153

As of yet, Susan's remains have not been located, nor have any other pieces of evidence.

Here are some of the popular theories regarding Susan's strange disappearance:

Susan became lost or injured and perished: In this wilderness area, it is very likely to become lost or injured. However, a major search of the area was conducted, and despite the fact that she was simply walking to a nearby meadow to watch birds, she was not hiking at all.

Susan met with foul play and was either abducted or murdered or both: The last person known to have seen Susan alive was the chef at base camp. Would it explain why no clothing or remains were found in the meadow if he had harmed her? Tom, her husband, is said to have possibly killed her when he found her, still watching birds, in the meadow while looking for her. However, no signs of an attack were discovered.

> Susan was killed and eaten by a wild animal: It could have been something akin to a mountain lion attack, but searchers found no signs of blood or ripped clothing, nor was there any sign of a struggle.

CONNIE MARIE JOHNSON – BIG FOG MOUNTAIN

CONNIE MARIE JOHNSON, seventy-six, worked as a camp cook for Richie Outfitters (based in Salmon, Idaho) in the area around Big Fog Mountain, near Big Rock and Grangeville in Idaho, in early October 2018. With no roads in the area, it could only be accessed on foot or by horseback.

On October 2, 2018, the hunters left the camp, and this is the last time she has been seen. Sheriff Doug Giddings reported that the hunters were able to radio Connie the next day, but their reception was too weak to understand her. Their return to the campsite on October 5 found Connie and Ace, her dog, gone.

She was also a former US Forest Service wilderness ranger at Moose Creek Ranger Station, where she gained a great deal of experience in the outdoors. She was also a member of the Selway-Bitterroot Foundation and led tours of the backcountry in that region for young people and other groups. Even if something went wrong, she knew how to survive in the backcountry, according to her friends.

Former colleague Chris Adkins says, "It's reconcilable. You know, what everyone is dealing with, with this, because like you said, this isn't like some pilgrim's first rodeo. This is a woman who spent literally the last twenty-five years of her life, most of them, on foot in the wilderness, alone, doing her wilderness range work, and if there's anybody that has a skill set that positions them to beat this, it's Connie."

Johnson talked about her experiences in the backcountry after relocating from Iowa several years earlier in an oral history she recorded for the Selway-Bitterroot Foundation:

"I don't remember really being afraid of anything. I'm a spiritual and faithful person and I kind of gave over my life to, you know, there's God taking care of me and I know that but I did learn to, and I don't remember being fearful. There were lightning storms and there were creek crossings and there were lots of challenging things physically, but I'm naturally an impatient person and this taught me, since I was by myself, to be very careful about where you put your feet. You know, Connie, if you

get hurt here there's no way anybody's going to help you; you're on your own. So it taught me to plan ahead about how I would negotiate this or that or how I would deal with the water supply or bee stings and that kind of thing. I just love being in that place so much. It just took care of me, you know. It's a pretty overpowering feeling to look up into those hills and especially being a flatlander like I was. I still am in awe of the power of those mountains and the power of the weather and the creeks and just the sheer hugeness of it and the fact that we're not in control of anything."

With blonde hair and blue eyes, she was five feet seven inches and 140 pounds.

The US Air Force, the Idaho National Guard and the Clearwater County Backcountry Helicopter Rescue team all deployed aircraft using FLIR heat technology to do a large search on foot and with tracking dogs. The search for Connie was ended on October 16, 2018, after no trace was found.

Three weeks later, the dog, Ace, turned up by himself at the Moose Creek ranger station, about half a mile from the camp. After the dog was examined and fed, it was taken out to maybe lead searchers to Connie. Unfortunately, this did not provide any additional clues as to the whereabouts of Connie.

Considering Connie's outdoor experience, what

happened to her in October 2018? Connie's survival skills were impeccable. She might have fallen ill or been in an accident. Is there another reason why she was not here?

Although her daughter could only speculate about what happened to her mother, she believed that it was not intentional that she disappeared. "I think that she was enjoying the outdoors, which she loves, and something happened."

As of this writing in November 2021, no trace of Connie Johnson has been found, and the case remains open and unsolved.

DEORR JAY KUNZ JR. – LEADORE, IDAHO

DEORR KUNZ JR., two years old at the time, from Idaho Falls, disappeared on July 10, 2015. His parents, Jessica Mitchell and Vernal DeOrr Kunz Senior, were with him at Timber Creek Campground, ten miles from Leadore (east of Challis), Idaho. Stone Reservoir was nearby, and a stream ran alongside the site.

The camping trip included DeOrr's great-grandfather (the grandfather of Jessica), Robert Walton, and Isaac Reinwand, Walton's friend.

When DeOrr went missing, it was the middle of the afternoon, and the group was on a fishing trip. Mitchell and Vernal's decision to take a camping and fishing trip, according to other family members, came as a surprise and was unexpected. Going into the wilderness would prove to be a fateful decision.

DeOrr Jr.'s parents believed that Robert Walton was watching him at the Timber Creek Campground, while the boy's great-grandfather believed he was with Isaac and his parents down by the creek. At the time of his disappearance, DeOrr was reportedly wearing a camouflage hoodie, blue pants, and oversized cowboy boots.

Separate 911 calls, police interviews, and other evidence led to an investigation that raised more questions than it answered.

Since then, DeOrr hasn't been seen, and no charges have been filed. They were named suspects in January 2016 by former Limhi County Sheriff Lynn Bowerman, but they were not charged or arrested. There was little evidence proving that they were involved in criminal activity.

It has been claimed by the parents that they have no idea what happened to their son from the start. When Reinwand and Walton were interviewed by the police, they said they had no idea where the boy was. In June 2019, Walton passed away, taking any knowledge he had of the incident to the grave.

Aside from ongoing litigation between the family and a private investigator, the case has been relatively quiet in recent months. A bone found at the campsite in June 2019 was not from the missing boy and was from an animal, according to the FBI's office in Quantico, Virginia.

Currently, the case is still active as of the time of this writing, according to Sheriff Steve Penner. In the wake of the 2017 election that saw Lynn Bowerman step down as Lemhi County's sheriff, Steve Penner is now in charge of this case both as lead investigator and also as county sheriff. The case is considered open and ongoing.

While the voluminous details of this case could easily fill an entire book, we may never know exactly what happened to little DeOrr or who is to blame.

TODD WILLIAM HOFFLANDER – WINDY SADDLE

TODD WILLIAM HOFFLANDER, thirty-nine, was last seen on Tuesday, September 27, 2010, in the Windy Saddle area of Idaho County, Idaho. A friend and he were hiking in Hells Canyon to the Snake River when they decided to separate and take different paths. His whereabouts are unknown; he is believed to have perished. It is believed that Todd's remains were discovered in April 2020, almost ten years after he died. DNA testing confirmed the remains were those of Todd Hofflander in late January 2021.

Todd's experience in Hells Canyon was indeed hellish.

In the area between Windy Saddle and McGaffee Cabin, Todd was helping some friends scout mule deer bucks. The group planned to hike for four days. The group split up on September 27, and Todd disappeared. McGaffee Cow Camp is the last location where he was seen.

With elevations varying from 8,000 to 1,500 feet above sea level in short distances, the terrain is rough and steep. During his hike, he was accompanied by his dog Ruby, a black Labrador retriever.

Hoffmann lived in Lucile, Idaho, when he went missing. Hoffmann was an experienced hiker who was sufficiently prepared for an overnight experience. A pistol with five bullets, unknown caliber, was in his possession. Also in his backpack were a Bic lighter, Lipton red beans and rice, three jugs of water, two cans of chicken, chewy bars and pots, and a bright red sleeping bag that would keep him warm in temperatures as low as 15 degrees Fahrenheit. The weight of his pack is estimated to have been fifty pounds, at a minimum. There was no radio or cell phone with him. Ruby the dog wore a red backpack made just for canines.

Todd wore a green T-shirt with a white design on the front, blue jeans, a blue baseball cap, size 10 Asolo hiking boots, and a gold wedding band. The backpack he was carrying was camouflage-printed. The man had a mustache, a goatee, and scars from previous piercings in his left ear, scars on his groin, on his backbone, and on the side of his head at the temple. He had several tattoos, including a portrait of Jesus with the word "SAVES" on his right chest, a bison skull on the left side, cartoon character Wile

E. Coyote on his right bicep, an eagle on his left, a small circle between his right thumb and index finger, and the word "KING" across his back and "THUG LIFE" across his lower abs.

In the afternoon of September 28, 2010, when Todd hadn't shown up, his friends called the authorities, who launched a search and rescue operation. A helicopter from Hillcrest Aircraft Company and Back Country Medics from Orofino assisted in the search early on. In addition to Bernard Creek, Bills Creek, Lightning Creek, the east and west branches of Sheep Creek, McCaffee Basin, and Bear Basin, the aircraft conducted grid searches. Additionally, dog teams from the search and rescue teams of Idaho and Clearwater Counties were involved.

Heaven's Gate Lookout was the site of an Incident Command post manned by deputies from Idaho and Clearwater Counties. A thorough search turned up no sign of the missing person.

Several days after the disappearance, Ruby, the dog, was found in the woods, dehydrated, but otherwise in good shape, after a fruitless search for Todd. Approximately fifteen miles south of Riggins, on Seven Devils Road, was where Ruby was located. Hofflander was last seen on the opposite side of the Seven Devil Mountain range from where she was found. There was no success in getting her to lead them to Todd. As searchers combed the area near the dog's location, they came up empty-handed.

According to Todd's wife, the hunting party split up because the husband's knee was bothering him. They were supposed to meet down at the river, but the husband never showed up. The others believed he could make it on his own, so they left him behind. She further added that her husband may have become confused because of the injury when he started making his way toward the meeting place.

A hunter found what appeared to be the remains of a human skull above Bernard Creek on Sunday, April 26, 2020, according to the Idaho County Sheriff's Office and Idaho County Coroner's Office. The hunter found camping equipment and a digital camera as well in the area.

Killgore Adventures took eight Idaho County Sheriff's Office personnel by jet boat to the mouth of Bernard Creek. They walked about a mile into the area, finding human skeletal remains and a portion of a skull. In addition, hunting gear and a pack belonging to Hofflander was identified by his wife.

Photographs from an SD card found inside the pack, belonging to Hofflander, were recovered by officers. Authorities said that everything found at the scene pointed to Todd's remains. For evaluation and DNA testing, Idaho County Coroner Cody Funke sent the bones to the Ada County Coroner in Boise.

According to County Coroner Cody Funke, the human remains that were discovered in the area of the Seven Devils and Bernard Creek in April 2020 have been positively identified as Todd Hofflander. DNA analysis was used by the FBI to identify the remains.

So what are we to believe happened to Todd Hofflander? Did his injury cause him to stumble? When he left the rest of his hunting group, how did he end up so far away from the point he left? Was Todd's disappearance somehow connected to his friends? Despite Ruby being discovered alive, how had she become separated from Todd, or what caused her to leave him? If only Ruby could talk...

TERRENCE SHEMEL WOODS JR. – PENMAN MINE

TERRENCE SHEMEL WOODS, twenty-seven, a freelance filmmaker, was part of a production crew recording a reality show at Penman mine in western Idaho on October 5, 2018. Terrence jumped off a cliff and dashed into the dense mountain forest as the crew was wrapping up, stunning them all. Terrence had disappeared before anyone could react.

Approximately fifty-six miles to the north, Connie Johnson disappeared in mysterious circumstances from Fog Mountain in Idaho.

Another missing person was reported to the Idaho County Sheriff's Office around 5:30 p.m. on Sunday, October 7. Jose Mendez-Morales, forty-two, left Tacoma, Washington, and was heading to Elk City, Idaho. His family last heard from him on September 25 in

Grangeville, but he has not been in touch since. His routine is to check in every three days or roughly thereabouts. A red and white Ford F-250 with Washington license plate A84361P is believed to be driven by José.

The Penman mine is located within the Nez Perce–Clearwater National Forest's Orogrande area. The area is located in Idaho County in Western Idaho's mountainous region of 8,500 square miles. There are four separate wilderness areas within the 2,224,091-acre Nez Perce National Forest, located in west-central Idaho.

A national forest that lies in the heart of north-central Idaho, Nez Perce–Clearwater National Forest is located there. On the west, it crosses the Oregon border, on the east it crosses the Montana border, on the north it crosses the Idaho Panhandle National Forest and on the south, it crosses the Salmon River. The county is situated in the counties of Latah, Nez Perce, Idaho, Clearwater, and Lewis.

The forest was traditionally home to the Ni Mii Puu, who were later named the Nez Perce Indians by Lewis and Clark. When the forests were administratively combined in 2012, the name Nez Perce–Clearwater National Forests was chosen to honor the Nez Perce Tribe.

Executive Order No. 854 signed by President Theodore Roosevelt created the Nez Perce National Forest. In that order, which became effective on July 1, 1908, the Bitter Root and Weiser National Forests gave up lands to establish the forest. By Executive Order No. 6889, part of Selway National Forest was added on October 29, 1934.

President Theodore Roosevelt signed Executive Order No. 842 creating the Clearwater National Forest. The Coeur d'Alene National Forest and Bitterroot National Forest contributed lands to create the forest pursuant to Order no. 186, which took effect on July 1, 1908. Selway National Forest was expanded by Executive Order No. 6889 on October 29, 1934.

Mountain wildlife in this forest includes timber wolves, raccoons, moose, black bears, coyotes, cougars, and elk.

It is very mountainous in the five-to-seven-thousand-foot range and extremely dense with large deadfall trees, making travel by foot difficult in certain areas.

Terry was raised in Capitol Heights, Maryland, with his parents and three siblings. He graduated from the University of Maryland. Having studied at the American International University in London for several years, he returned to the US in 2018. As an experienced journalist, he filmed documentaries and television shows around the world in difficult conditions.

He has never experienced panic attacks or psychiatric difficulties such as depression, according to his father.

During the wilderness shoot, he appeared well prepared. After his disappearance, his parents were given his backpack. It contained two camera bags, batteries, Sharpies, over-the-counter painkillers, cough drops, hand cream, a phone charger, a folding tactical knife, and a stun gun. It is unclear why he would leave all of these things at the site.

In addition to Turkey and Alaska, he had been on several rustic wilderness shoots before this, so he has experience in the backcountry and this area of Idaho, but not in the mining area.

Text messages sent before he left indicate that he didn't want to take the trip. The comments were not shocking to friends, but they thought they were unusual afterward. He was said to have behaved differently on this shoot than he normally would.

After searching for seven days, the Idaho County Sheriff's Department began to scale back the search on 10/11/18 when Terrence's body had not been found.

Law enforcement officials reportedly went to the room of the suspect to ensure that it was locked at one point during the search. However, it was revealed that some members of the crew had already been in his room to get items for the tracking dogs.

Additionally, the news media reported that law enforcement never requested Terrence's cell phone records or searched Terrence's laptop for any history. Each would have required going to a judge and getting a subpoena, which would have required evidence of a crime or that he was in danger. Investigators determined that Terrence wanted to disappear. However, no subpoena was issued. In cases like this, getting the appropriate authority to conduct the searches would not have been difficult.

The sheriff said that the people working the SAR operation are confident that Terrence was not in this area when they searched. He made his way to the road after sliding down the bank. After that, they are unsure where he went. If he had been injured, they feel they would have found him, and if he had taken his own life, then the dogs would have discovered him.

Another officer, however, expressed shock at his ability to leave. Over the years, deadfall lodgepoles and Douglas firs have piled up on top of one another on the forest floor. Running through giant pickup sticks accompanied by areas so thick with deadfall your feet would not touch the ground was how the officer described it.

Also, no prints or other evidence of Terrence were found in the fresh snow.

Theories abound as to what became of Terrence. Let's look at a couple of them. In the opinion of law enforcement, what happened was possibly:

He suffered a mental breakdown or panic attack. There is conflicting information regarding this. Before his disappearance, some reports reported that he had been detained, but later reports said he was debriefed about wildlife in the area rather than detained. Law enforcement said he wanted to disappear.

There are only sixteen thousand people in this area, based on the sheriff's estimate of two people per square mile and 8,500 square miles. This makes for a very large, unpopulated area where you can easily go missing if that were desired.

According to family and friends, the following could

have happened:

As the production crew and sheriff's office were very unhelpful, the parents suspect foul play. There is speculation that he was in an uncomfortable situation and trying to escape. His parents suggested that race may have been involved. His father mentioned this on a radio program. By email, Terrence's detective explicitly denied the role of race in the investigation. Additionally, the detective stated they would no longer be communicating with his father.

The older sister of Terrence Woods, Sharnia Tisdale, describes her brother as a bright and ambitious man with a kind and loving heart, claiming that the activity the Idaho County Police described was completely out of character for Terrence.

For now, we can only speculate what happened and where Terrence went when he disappeared.

JO ELLIOTT-BLAKESLEE & AMY LINKERT – CRATERS OF THE MOON NATIONAL MONUMENT

DR. JODEAN "JO" Kay Elliott-Blakeslee, sixty-three, worked at the Snake River Correctional Institution in Ontario, Oregon, and Amelia "Amy" Linkert, sixty-nine, had retired from her position at Lowell Scott Middle School.

The two women traveled to the Craters of the Moon National Monument and Preserve from Boise, Idaho, on September 13, 2013. The two women never returned. When they visited the monument, they encountered jagged rocks and stormy weather. So what really happened to Jo and Amy at the famous Idaho destination? Is a misadventure really all that happened in the lava fields, or is there something else going on, perhaps something sinister?

On May 2, 1924, the Craters of the Moon National Monument and Preserve was established in the Snake River Plain in central Idaho. In between the small towns of Arco and Carey, it lies along US 20 (which is concurrent with US 93 and US 26) at an average elevation of 5,900 feet (1,800 m). A considerable portion of the park's features are volcanic, and it is one of the best-preserved flood basalt areas on the continent.

As part of a presidential proclamation signed by President Clinton in November 2000, the monument area was greatly expanded. In August 2002, the 410,000-acre portion of the expanded monument was designated as Craters of the Moon National Preserve by the National Park Service.

An estimated 1,117 square miles (2,893 km²) of the area consists of lava fields and sagebrush steppe grasslands covering about 400 square miles.

On Friday, September 20, 2013, Jo and Amy failed to return as planned from their trip to the Craters of the Moon National Monument in Idaho.

On Tuesday, September 24, they were reported missing. As soon as Dr. Jo failed to show up for work, her employees called the police. At the time, the federal government was shut down due to funding issues, so the search was delayed almost a week. In the days before the official search began, ten park service rangers searched on foot for Jo and Amy without access to any government resources, such as helicopters or planes.

On September 19, they were seen at a campground in Arco, which is about eighteen miles away from Craters. Craters of the Moon visitors' center receipts indicate that they were at the monument on Tuesday, September 24, according to police.

A popular trailhead in the monument, the Tree Molds Trail parking lot, was later found to contain their vehicle. In an unexpected turn of events, the pickup truck at the trailhead contained the women's dogs, cell phones, and other items. It seems that they weren't planning to stay away very long if they left their dogs behind.

Due to the presence of their dogs, Jo and Amy's family said they would not go off trail. Tammy Kerklow, Amy's niece, said, "They were both missionaries, they're both avid hikers, survivalists, this is very strange. To have their phones, I mean I know they probably wouldn't work in the caves but to leave them in the truck, that's strange to us."

With this in mind, the search and rescue team conducted its search. A five-square-mile area was searched near the Tree Molds, Broken Top Loop, and Wilderness Trails on the south end of the monument. Weather and terrain were unpredictable in the search area, which was in rugged and often dangerous territory. Even after six thousand volunteer hours of searching, they failed to locate them.

On September 25, 2013, search and rescue teams expanded the search area and found Amy Linkert's body in the lava field northwest of Tree Molds Trail.

Facedown on the lava, she was only wearing a short-sleeve shirt and pants, without a backpack, jacket, food, or even water to drink. Her death was believed to be caused by exposure after she became disoriented while searching for help. Police did not suspect foul play. The searchers originally believed they had found Jo since there was no identification on the body, but dental records proved that the body belonged to Amy.

In October 2013, searchers finally found Jo about a mile from Amy's body after spending an extra month on the search. The body was two and a half miles from the pickup and was obscured by rocks in an area where search helicopters had been flying for the past month.

In both cases, the women appeared to have died from exposure, as well as showing signs of being severely dehydrated. However, it is unclear why they were separated and how they died. Perhaps one of the women sustained an injury, and the other woman went to seek assistance and had an encounter of her own.

Several questions remain unanswered in this case:

Did Jo and Amy intend to stay in the area if they left their dogs and cell phones in the pickup? Around the time the two women were visiting the monument, a storm hit the area around it. Did the storm cause them to panic and become disorientated?

The reason Amy was found facedown on the lava without a jacket, backpack, food, or water is unclear. Why did she take the trail without any gear? Because the dogs were left in the vehicle, it is clear that the visit was intended as a short hike. Did it really come down to the weather changing? Possibly.

What caused Jo and Amy to separate? Was one of them hurt by the jagged lava rocks in the area before the other?

In spite of numerous helicopter flyovers, why was Jo's body found so far from the trailhead car park, and why did it take so long to find her body? Body parts can get obscured by the rocks, which can take a long time to find, so that explanation is kind of understandable.

However, it seems unlikely that the two just left their dogs behind and wandered about in this potentially dangerous terrain without supplies, even if the authorities have dismissed foul play. The pickup truck was left behind, but what led to their separation? In addition to being keen hikers and survivalists, the family member described them as being both knowledgeable about wilderness areas and not naive or ignorant. The Craters of the Moon National Monument provides a stunning backdrop for the sad end of these women's lives. May they rest in peace.

SEVEN
HAUNTED IDAHO

Brig and Campgrounds, Farragut State Park
13550 ID-54, Athol, ID 83801
(208) 683-2425
https://parksandrecreation.idaho.gov/parks/farragut/

In this small museum, which was formerly a jail for misbehaving recruits, a few of the cells have been preserved. By nightfall, the compound is filled with distant yells and cell clinking.

Strange orbs and faces seen peering through bars have been reported. In a local legend, a German prisoner was captured and killed on the lower floor, and his body was left to decompose in unrest for all time.

Among the array of sculptures within the museum area, one stands out in particular—a sailor bust embellished with the memories of former recruits. Visitors report seeing this stone face moving and shifting as though it were trying to remove itself.

On the beach, random sightings of men wearing uniforms have been reported.

There is no way to know who (or what) haunts the campsites and the park. Could it be the ghosts of former sailors? Perhaps revengeful prisoners? Or perhaps something else? There is no denying the historical significance of Farragut... or that nightfall is not the best time to explore the woods.

Almost everyone who stays overnight at Farragut and heads to Silverwood the next morning doesn't realize that they are sleeping in an active paranormal campsite... until something strange happens.

Bear River Massacre
US Highway 91, Preston, ID

JANUARY 1863 MARKED the beginning of everything. From Fort Douglas in Salt Lake City, Utah, Colonel Connor led a group of California volunteers to the present-day Preston, Idaho, area.

They were looking for Shoshone tribal members. The members of this tribe were accused of attacking settlers.

Colonel Connor, accompanied by his men, attacked the winter camp of Chief Bear Hunter at Battle Creek early on the morning of January 29, 1863. Around four

NATIONAL PARK MYSTERIES AND DISAPPEARANCES   175

hundred men, women, and children from the tribe were savagely killed.

There are harrowing stories of Native Americans hiding from the soldiers, jumping into freezing rivers in order to escape, and tales almost too horrible to imagine.

A monument stands where you can pay tribute to those who died during this terrible event, and there are several markers telling the story. A prayer tree can also be found here. Various items have been tied to this tree to remember those who passed away many years ago.

Yankee Fork State Park
24424 State Hwy 75, Challis, ID 83226
https://parksandrecreation.idaho.gov/parks/land-yankee-fork/

HERE IS the story of the Bulgarian monk of Yankee Fork, who has been reported as being a spirit or ghost and haunting the vicinity.

The area was home to a Bulgarian monk from about the 1870s to the 1890s, which is when he was reported to have drowned. There are stories that he traveled and gave lectures. There are stories that he was seen playing with children twenty-five miles away on the day he drowned. Witnesses have reported seeing the black-robed figure wandering along the riverbanks at night with a lantern ever since.

Rose Hill Cemetery
2355 Rollandet St, Idaho Falls, ID 83402

THOSE WHO KNOCK on a certain aboveground tomb, a square monument, will hear its ghostly occupant knocking back. Another legend describes two gravesites that once stood side by side. The first bore the name Wear, while the second bore the name Wolff. Due to the tales of werewolves that followed, the graves in question have been moved within the cemetery.

Massacre Rocks State Park
3592 W Park St, American Falls, ID 83211
https://parksandrecreation.idaho.gov/parks/massacre-rocks/

WATER BABIES HAVE a reputation for kidnapping children and devouring them in cold blood, one of the most feared supernatural stories of all time. These creatures are believed to dwell in Massacre Rocks State Park and Fort Hall Bottoms, which are now off-limits.

An account tells of a famine that afflicted Native Americans along the Snake River. In what they thought was a mass mercy killing, they drowned their children collectively to spare their children from starvation. Others claim that white pioneers committed the act while traveling across the hot, barren landscape of Idaho.

Plaza Bridge
North Plaza Road, Emmett, ID

IN THE SOUTHERN part of Idaho, Emmett is a charming little rural town. The population is around 6,500, and life here is easy. Although the town is known for its agriculture, it is also considered a paranormal hotspot and even has a haunted bridge.

Known as the "Plaza Bridge," it is located along North Plaza Road. It is not uncommon to see kids of all ages jumping off the bridge into the river below during the summer. Cool off at this place when it's hot, but don't stick around if it gets dark.

There is a great deal of mystery surrounding this creepy legend. Paranormal events, however, attest to this legend's authenticity. Many weird occurrences have been described by witnesses, but one of the most common is an apparition of a woman seemingly searching for her child. While the woman searches, the wailing of a baby can sometimes be heard.

Several years ago, paranormal investigators in the town conducted a ghost hunt. The apparition of three child spirits that floated in front of their car was accompanied by a mysterious white mist. The most unsettling part of this story is that an EVP was recorded that told the group to get back in their vehicles and leave.

The tents of people who have camped in the area have also been scratched and tapped by fingernails. This bridge seems haunted by something that hasn't yet proven to be harmful. Nevertheless, its presence is unsettling.

Lava Hot Springs Inn & Spa
1 Center St, Lava Hot Springs, ID 83246
(208) 776-5830
http://www.lavahotspringsinn.com/

IN THE QUIET town of Lava Hot Springs, this inn has quite a history, and its reputation has brought a lot of attention. A television show about ghost hunting even featured the hotel. In this haunted hotel, there's no doubt that there is something strange going on.

In today's world, the inn looks much like an old hospital or sanatorium. After all, it was a hospital and a sanatorium for a long time. During the 1980s, the building was transformed into a hotel after serving as a hospital for decades.

Built in the late 1930s, the hospital served as a rehab center for injured soldiers during World War II. After the war, it served as a home for elderly patients in the county. It is still inhabited by a lot of these patients—or at least their spirits.

It is said that room 13 is the "most haunted" room in the hotel, so you might want to challenge yourself to spend the night there if you are into paranormal experiences. When guests stay in the room, they often see an apparition of a woman named Martha.

Usually, Martha's presence in the room wakes people up. Her trademark question is, "What are you doing here?" She appears to wear a hospital gown and can sometimes be observed peering out the window or doing what appears to be sewing or knitting.

The second-floor sitting room in the hotel was once the operating room of the hospital, which may be interesting (or just plain spooky). Room 13 was the anesthesia area used to prepare patients for surgery.

Aside from room 13, the building has many haunted rooms. It is known that the ghost of an old World War II soldier can be seen in room 7, and the ghost of an old angry lady can be seen in room 10. The hospital turned out to be home to many of its patients for life and the afterlife as well.

Guests at the hotel report hearing disembodied voices, phantom footsteps in empty corridors, water faucets that turn off and on by themselves, and other strange phenomena. Hotel staff members have assured guests, however, that there has been no malicious activity reported by guests.

Spirit Lake
Kootenai County, ID
https://www.spiritlakeid.gov/

DESPITE IDAHO'S reputation as a haunted state, the state's most haunted places are much less well-known than our neighbors'—but if you know how to find them, you can find them. There are many eerie stories that are told around these hotbeds of paranormal activity, passed down from generation to generation, and they are often attributed to Native Americans.

This foggy, densely forested lake is surrounded by densely forested mountains, which is why it's considered one of Idaho's spookiest places.

Spirit Lake is one of only two lakes in the world with an entirely sealed bottom—meaning phantom spirits and earthly souls are said to wander its shores.

As legend has it, once the lake was called "Clear Water," but the Kootenai Indians who once lived on its shores suffered a tragedy that resulted in its new name: "Tesemini," meaning "Lake of Spirits."

The legend of Hya-Pam, the daughter of a Kootenai chief, follows her love affair with Hasht-Eel-Ame-Hoom (Shining Eagle), a fearless young Kootenai warrior. However, Hya-Pam's father consented to a peace marriage with a chieftain of a rival tribe in order to avoid war.

Nevertheless, the two young lovers vowed to be together forever. As they bound themselves, they dove into the lake.

It is said that on moonlit nights, when the wind is still, you can see their ghostly silhouettes as they drift along in a phantom canoe in the middle of the lake.

A low, mournful, and haunting sound drifts through the mist that hangs over the water every spring. Many think the voices are actually the cries of the Native American lovers trying to escape the Lake of the Spirits. However, it never happens.

IN CLOSING

That's it for another volume of *National Park Mysteries &
Disappearances,* we hope you enjoyed it and discovered
new information.

The wilderness of the Pacific Northwest and all its
splendor are many things... expansive, beautiful, and a
popular destination for tourists. Yet, it can also be frightening, dangerous, and downright deadly to those unfortunate
enough to be in the wrong place at the wrong time.

With all that said, we truly do not wish to discourage
anyone from visiting these strange and wonderful places.
Just keep these stories in mind, stay safe, stay alive, and
come back with a camera full of pictures, a head full of
strange and beautiful encounters, and feel proud that you
lived to tell the tale.

Thank you for reading this book. We look forward to
telling more tales of other national parks—many of which
are just as weird and fascinating. In the meantime, be good

IN CLOSING

to yourselves and each other, and we'll talk to you next time. Be well and be blessed.

—Steve

Enjoyed this series?
Check out Steve's, *LEGENDS & STORIES* series.
LEGENDS AND STORIES: FROM THE APPALACHIAN TRAIL

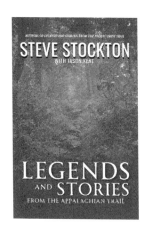

ABOUT THE AUTHOR

Steve Stockton is a veteran outdoorsman and author who has been investigating the unexplained for over 35 years. Originally from the mountains of East Tennessee, Steve has traveled all over the country and many parts of the world and now makes his home in picturesque New England with his wife, Nicole, and their dog, Mulder.

Steve cites his influences as his "gypsy witch" grandmother, who told him multitudes of legends and stories as a small child, as well as authors such as Frank Edwards, John Keel, Charles Fort, Loren Coleman, Ivan Sanderson, Colin Wilson, and Nick Redfern.

His published books include Strange Things in the Woods (a collection of true, paranormal encounters) as well as the autobiographical My Strange World, where he talks about his own experiences dating back to childhood. Recently, he has written National Park Mysteries and Disappearances, Volumes 1, 2, and 3.

He also owns and narrates the wildly popular Among The Missing Youtube channel.

ALSO BY STEVE STOCKTON

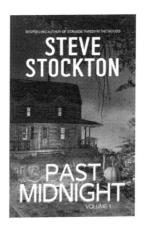

13 PAST MIDNIGHT SERIES

MYSTERIES IN THE DARK SERIES

STRANGE THINGS IN THE WOODS

MY STRANGE WORLD

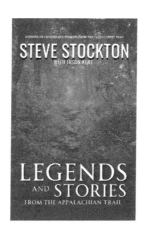

LEGENDS AND STORIES: FROM THE APPALACHIAN TRAIL